Sports Cars 1928-39

Cars of the World in Colour

SPORTS CARS
1928—39

by
T. R. NICHOLSON

Illustrated by
JOHN W. WOOD

LONDON
BLANDFORD PRESS

First published in 1969
copyright © 1969 Blandford Press Ltd.
167 High Holborn, London W.C.1

SBN 7137 0060 2

ACKNOWLEDGEMENTS

The author and the publishers are grateful to the following, who comprise the
many *marque* specialists who kindly read proofs and suggested alterations, and
others who provided data and references:
M. F. L. Allison; R. O. Barnard; E. A. Bellamy; Lt. Col. C. H. D. Berthon;
Charles L. Betts Jr.; Anthony Bird; Antony Blight; John Bolster; Robert Burrows;
H. G. Conway; Dudley Coram; J. R. Davy; K. R. Day; Ian Dussek; J. O. Dyson;
D. C. Field; B. W. Garrett; G. N. Georgano; Peter Hull; Denis Jenkinson;
William C. Kinsman; G. Lancaster-Jones; Barrie McKenzie; Cyril Posthumus;
The Royal Automobile Club Library; Desmond Peacock; E. A. Price; David
Scott-Moncrieff; Michael Sedgwick; J. Stoton; R. L. Sutherland; David Thirlby;
The Veteran Car Club of Great Britain; Michael Wilby.

Colour section printed by Colour Reproduction Ltd, Billericay
Text printed in Great Britain by
Richard Clay (The Chaucer Press) Ltd, Bungay, Suffolk

INTRODUCTION

The sports car defies definition. It is a hybrid. It has enjoyed its success because it has part of the romance of the pure racing car, and something of the practical attainability of the family sedan. It is a specialized, limited machine, and it is every man's toy. Let us look at its development in outline until the end of the 1920s, and in more detail over the following decade.

The sports car had no single origin. The lines of development began in different countries at different times, for different reasons. Some were dead-ends, such as the sporting versions of the minimal form of motoring in the 1910–20 period, the cycle-car; or of the typical French small car or *voiturette* of the decade that followed. Other lines grew and flourished, as we shall see. The name 'sports car' was not invariably used; 'fast tourer' was common. Whichever word was used, it could mean different things, according to the will of the manufacturer or the fashion of the time or of the country, and could have different purposes. Even today, in an age of increasing rationalization, there is a choice of types and meanings, from the sports car for the unsporting motorist who is trying to look sporting, to the GT (Grand Touring) car that was evolved when sports cars for speed competition developed so far that they became almost indistinguishable from Grand Prix cars.

In its earliest forms, the sports car derived from the demands of competitions. Racing cars of the turn of the century were only just beginning to differ from touring cars. In 1898 a motorist of sporting inclinations, by simply removing wings and lamps, could convert his Panhard-Levassor, if it was one of the more powerful models, or (in 1903) his Mercedes Sixty, from a perfectly practical touring car into an equally useful racer. In that such machines were road cars suited to a motorist of sporting habits, they were sports cars according to one definition. Soon thereafter, compromises began to be deliberately built for these motorists, keeping pace with the increasing technical sophistication of pure racing cars and thus, *ipso facto*, growing away from the touring car. Such machines were the 60 h.p. De Dietrich of 1905, the 1906 60/80 h.p. Métallurgique from Belgium, and the overhead-camshaft KM and TM Isotta-Fraschinis of 1910–13. By the end of that period, vehicles of this kind were obsolete dinosaurs, because touring cars and racing cars had drawn far apart; the compromises were not fast enough for serious racing at Grand Prix level. Grand Prix cars were now highly specialized, complex thoroughbreds such as the Henry-designed Peugeots, with which no compromise could compete. The latter's sketchy two-passenger bodywork rendered them unsuitable for normal use. Anyway, as will be seen, other lines of development were already flourishing, deriving from touring cars rather than racing cars, not attempting to compete with the latter, but evolving into classes of their own.

In the U.S.A. by 1914, the American type of sports car was formed, and would not radically change until it died twenty years later. It was a distinct type on its own, not a dual-purpose car or a compromise like its European counterparts. As a type, the speedster was not regarded as a serious racing car, since its mechanical components were usually based firmly on those of touring cars made by the same manufacturer, which were almost invariably of extremely orthodox design; and it was certainly not suited to touring, with its absolute minimum of bodywork, consisting generally of no more than two bucket seats with a bolster fuel tank behind, wings, and perhaps a tiny 'monocle'-type windshield. The speedster had sporting looks, and a performance which likewise set it aside from its stodgier touring brethren, thanks to a combination of low weight, a big engine, and high gearing (Stutz Bearcat, Locomobile, Simplex, Mercer Type 35J Raceabout).

England and France inaugurated lines of development of their own, as well as sharing them. French small-car races, notably the Coupe des Voiturettes and Coupe de L'Auto series of 1906–14, gave rise to the sporting *voiturette*, a type derived from touring cars (Lion-Peugeot, Delage, Sizaire-Naudin, Hispano-Suiza) that was smaller and usually of simpler design than the machines just discussed, but were reflections in miniature of full-sized racing cars. More important for Britain (though she, too, took part in these French races) was the existence of Brooklands racetrack, opened in 1907, where racing and record-breaking produced sports cars or 'fast tourers' from Vauxhall, Austin, Sunbeam, Talbot, Straker-Squire, Crossley, and others. These were similar in character to, being developed from, the same firms' staid, medium-sized, middle-class touring cars. They generally had side-valve four-cylinder engines, mildly tuned, with lighter but still comfortable bodies and higher gearing. Their special virtue was stamina; i.e. sustained high-speed reliability, rather than outright speed. On the same lines were smaller machines in the light family-car class, with a cubic capacity of up to 2 litres. These cars set the pattern for the British sports

Fig. 1. Roots-type supercharger as used on Mercedes-Benz, Germany, *c.* 1929 (see 17)

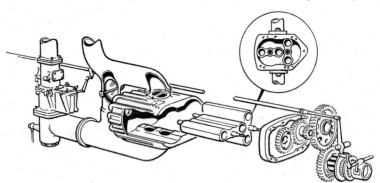

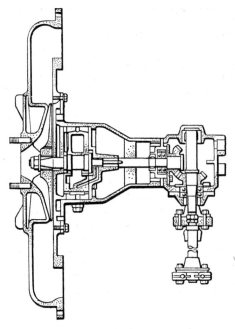

Fig. 2. Auburn supercharger, U.S.A., 1935 (see 66)

car until the late 1920s. From around 1910, another type of popular touring car was seen in sporting guise, the elementary cycle-car already mentioned (Bédélia, Violet-Bogey, GN, Buckingham), that originated in France. This normally consisted of an engine of motor-cycle type installed in a sketchy frame, with belt or chain transmission, brakes and steering of the vaguest sort, and an extremely draughty and cramped two-passenger body.

Germany and the Austro-Hungarian Empire, for their part, provided the most important branch of the family tree, in that their cars had the most influence on sports cars as a whole.

Their lineage was clear. They were produced by the Herkomer and Prince Henry Trials of Germany, between 1906 and 1910, and the Austrian Alpine Trials of 1910–14. The German events started as touring-car contests, in which sheer speed came to outweigh other considerations. This factor, limited to some extent by the Trials regulations, which sought always to maintain their character as touring-car tests, led to the uniting of complex, high-efficiency engines with light, spartan four-passenger bodywork. Until 1928 this recipe was the dominant one among the fastest sports cars of the world. The double overhead-camshaft Prince Henry

3

Austro-Daimler of 1910 was the outstanding example. Other cars of this kind were made by Opel, Horch, Mercedes and Benz in Germany, and by Puch and Laurin-Klement in the Austro-Hungarian Empire. To a much lesser extent, Britain, too, was influenced by the Prince Henry and Alpine recipe, producing the Prince Henry Vauxhall of 1910 and the Alpine Eagle Rolls-Royce of 1914, which brought together a typically British conventional engine and the new type of sporting body.

Thus, by 1914 the breed and its sub-species had evolved—beside the aristocrats, just described, were the tuned family touring cars specialized in by the British, the smaller sporting cycle-car or *voiturette* that had been born in France, and the American speedster.

The period until 1928 was one of the consolidation of the first type, and the decline or death of the rest. Chassis design stagnated, but engine design advanced, owing to wartime development of aero engines, from which car designers took the virtues of high power-to-weight ratio and high-speed reliability. Overhead-camshaft layouts, allowing inclined valves and efficiently-shaped combustion chambers, gained ground among the more expensive machinery, as did the use of light alloys to reduce weight and aid heat dissipation. In this period were born and flourished the Bentley from England, the French Lorraine-Dietrich, the German Mercedes-Benz S series, the Alfa-Romeo RLSS from Italy, and the Austro-Daimler Type ADMIII of Austria. Some cars of the breed lived on for a few years beyond the end of the period, and will be seen or described in

Fig. 3. Austro-Daimler ADR chassis, Austria, 1929 (see 18, 19)

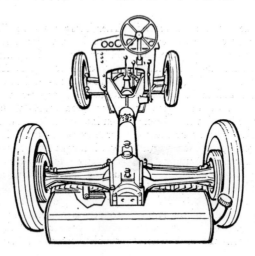

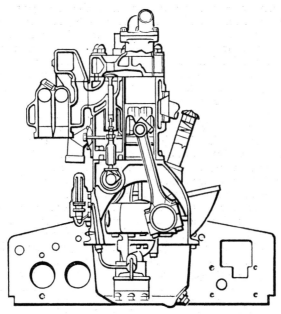

Fig. 4. Cord L-29 engine, U.S.A., 1929 (see 21)

this book (2, 17, 23, 24, 25). Their engines were usually of 3 litres' cubic capacity or more, installed in orthodox chassis that were fitted with the four-passenger bodies still demanded by the regulations of the most important sports-car competitions. This type ruled the racing circuits and the roads.

As before, France pursued her own lines of development as well. The most typical French sports car of the 1920s was the light sporting *voiturette*, descended from the pre-war Lion-Peugeots, Delages, etc. and also from the sporting cycle-car (which was dead by the early part of the decade). They generally had small four-cylinder en-gines of around 1 litre capacity, shaft drive, and very spartan bodywork. The best known were the Bugatti Type 13, the Amilcar, and the Salmson. France also produced a quite new departure, the semi-sporting tourer designed for high sustained cruising speeds (compared with the *voiturettes*) in reasonable comfort—high-geared, usually with an overhead valve, 2- to 3-litre engine, good brakes, and pleasant handling qualities, and wearing a light and elegant body. Such cars were the Ballot 2LT, the Delage DIS (9), and the Hotchkiss AM. They were a type designed for long-distance continental journeys over the good, straight roads that invited the motor-car now that it was reliable enough for such trips to be a matter of course.

Italy went the same way, with *voiturettes* (Ceirano, Chiribiri) and with its own fast tourers (Lancia Lambda, OM, Fiat 519, SPA, Itala, Ansaldo). Britain followed suit. However, her small sporting machines were mostly heavier, more comfortable, and less exciting than those of the Continent, for their pedigree was that of the family light car. In France, makers of this type stuck to their last, leaving the sporting small car to specialist manufacturers; in England, the latter was generally a not-much-modified version of the modest man's staid machine. Among them were the 14/28 MG, and the Hillman Speed Model. The outstanding exceptions were the Morgan three-wheeler, the GN cycle-car, and the latter's derivation, the Frazer Nash. The British fast tourer included a few survivals from the pre-war breed, such as the 30/98 h.p. Vauxhall, but most

were similar in character to those of Europe—Two Litre Lagonda (53), HE (26), Straker-Squire, Invicta (40), Alvis 12/50. The proven demand for all types of sports car was met by a proliferation of sports-car manufacturers and models. Most of the cars were either based on, and/or backed by, a range of bread-and-butter touring cars; few makers could specialize in sports cars alone. When they tried, such as Bentley (24, 25) and Aston Martin (56, 81), most found themselves in constant financial trouble, for the type was still of comparatively limited appeal.

All the different strains of sports car were encouraged by the multiplication of new sports-car races, in Britain, France, Italy, Belgium, and Germany. These were themselves a reflection of the growing popularity of the type. The most important and influential event was undoubtedly the Le Mans 24-hour Race. Close behind were the Coupe Boillot and the Bol d'Or, also held in France; the Belgian 24-hour Race at

Fig. 5. Alvis front-wheel drive chassis, Great Britain, 1929, plan (see 29)

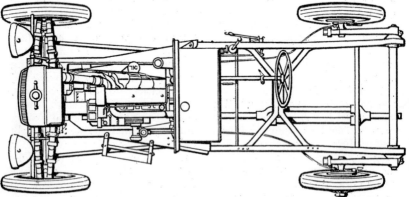

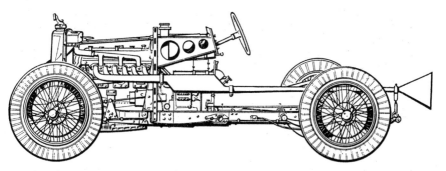

Fig. 6. MG K3 Magnette chassis, Great Britain, 1933–4, elevation (see 60)

Spa, Italy's Mille Miglia, and the Brooklands Double 12-hour Race and Tourist Trophy in Britain. Most attracted international entries.

In the U.S.A. in the early 1920s, the speedster became less fierce and stark, in response to the growing American demand for comfort and ease of driving, and for conventional conformity. The word 'sport' became more popular as the type of car it was applied to became less sporting. A 'sport' car meant that the speedster, or (a growing fad) the touring car decked out in sporty accessories, was used not as a car for taking part in competitions, but as a complement to other sporting activities —in which to go yachting, or horse racing, or (particularly) to play golf. The American equivalent of the optional close-ratio gear-box was the fitted golf bag. There was no sports-car racing in America to encourage the development of the true sports car. As before, too, the speedster or sports car was intended to enable its driver to cut a dash, to prove his individuality, to invest him (or her) with an aura of romance. The publicist and motor manufacturer Edward S. Jordan was the first man fully to exploit its possibilities in this direction. Among the best-known speedsters were Stutz, Paige, and Kissel.

The end of the 1920s—the beginning of the period covered in this book— brought three new trends. One was short-lived. From around 1928, and until they were strangled by the Depression around 1933, there arose a line of small, two-passenger sports cars of advanced engine design (though conventional chassis design), with a hitherto unparalleled power output for their modest cubic capacity, light in weight, and with superb handling qualities. They were bred for the competitions mentioned. Some were descended from touring types, but bore little resemblance to them in their behaviour. They were made in comparatively small numbers, and were very expensive compared with family cars. Before they died, indeed by 1930, they had successfully (aided by favourable handicapping) killed off the old breed of bigger, heavier, less stable sports cars that had hitherto dominated the

7

circuits. This type was by then already itself in full retreat before the onset of the Depression, for it, too, was a luxury that could be dispensed with. Among the giant-killers were the Alfa-Romeo 6C and 8C (42, 51), the Bertelli Aston Martins (56), the Riley Brooklands (27), and the Maserati 8C 1100 (50).

A second trend began to appear in the early 1930s. By this time, the possibilities of fast long-distance touring on the Continent had grown further with the opening of Italy's first *autostrade* and Germany's pioneer *autobahnen*. The comparatively cramped and noisy open fast tourers of the 1920s gave way to high-speed luxury cars, superbly built and finished, relying for their appeal on their extreme comfort, silence, and flexibility. They were designed for extended, effortless straight-line cruising, usually with big engines turning at a leisurely pace thanks to high gearing. Two-speed rear axles providing overdrive top were common in the type, as were pre-selector gear-boxes. These cars were usually based on the firm's luxury town-car chassis, but this was customarily a low-geared affair swamped by monumental perpendicular bodywork of a formal nature. The bodies of the new type, their most distinctive feature, may not always have been handsome, and they were generally heavy and not very roomy, but they could be surpassingly elegant and dashing, and were invariably eye-catching, with their low roof lines, long hoods, big trunks, and flowing lines with a horizontal emphasis.

Fig. 7. Mercedes-Benz Type 380K front suspension, Germany, 1932–3 (see 90)

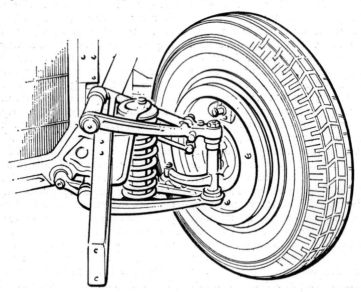

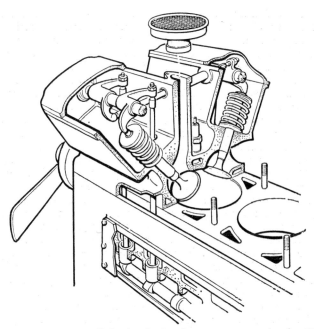

Fig. 8. BMW Type 328 cylinder-head, showing transverse pushrods, Germany, 1936–40 (see 75)

Like some of the cheap British vehicles to be described in a moment, and the American speedster, their status as sports cars is arguable. But they certainly had outright speed and acceleration which put many true sports cars to shame, some handled equally well, and their engine and chassis design, if not revolutionary, was generally very modern. A few, such as the British Talbot (49) and to a lesser extent the Bentley and the Hotchkiss (64, 80), could be developed into competition cars that were formidable by any standards. To beg the question, perhaps, the type looked the part when wearing sporting bodies, and were often called sports cars by their manufacturers. There is enough justification for including them here for, as has been pointed out, the sports car has had many origins and guises, and therefore as many definitions. Some of the most distinguished of the new 'transcontinental expresses' were the Talbot 105 and 110 (49), the Minerva AKS and 28CV (36), the Paris–Nice and Grand Sport Hotchkiss (80), the Continental Phantom II Rolls-Royce (34), the Rolls-Royce-built Bentley (64), the Speed Twenty Alvis and its successors (54), the Delage D8 (45), and the Mercedes-Benz 500K and 540K (90).

The third trend, that began to manifest itself about 1928, was far and away the most important and long-lasting in its effects. Its theme was sports cars for the masses. Earlier low-priced sports cars of the more serious sort were derived from the cycle-car or the pre-war *voiturette*, and were uncomfortable, often temperamental and hard to drive, and not cheap enough. The really cheap, and also reasonably comfortable sports car first appeared around 1928 in Britain (MG M-type Midget [39] etc.). These features guaranteed its acceptance in a wide market that was not interested in competition successes except vicariously. What was wanted was a car that looked and sounded the part, superficially at least. The most successful cars commercially were based on an established line of family cars, sharing its parts and service facilities. Still, when talking of sports cars based on mass-produced components and attracting a far wider market than hitherto, it is important to remember that they were still a minority interest. The most popular British machine was the MG M-type Midget, of which around 3200 were built in four years. Its touring parent, the overhead-camshaft Morris Minor, achieved around 34,500 units. For all their fame, production of the Alfa-Romeo 6C 1750 totalled 2591, Only 900 of the Fiat 508S were made, in five years, compared with 80,000 of the popular small car on which it was based, the Balilla 508. Of the Mercedes-Benz S series, 300 were made; of the BMW 328, 462; of the supercharged 4½-litre Bentley and S-type Invicta, 50 each; and of the Duesenberg SJ, about 36. Exactly ten Squires saw the light. On such figures are romantic reputations built—not commercial empires. As might be expected, technical advance was not a characteristic of the new breed, at least as far as the normal production of sports cars were concerned (much fiercer, serious competition cars based on these were catalogued, and offered in small numbers at high prices. They were a very different proposition). The British type was usually heavy, low-geared not only because of this but also to facilitate participation in road trials. It had a long-stroke engine (for tax reasons) of up to 1½ litres' cubic capacity, and the poor weight distribution and flexible frame of its touring brethren, which did not make for safe high-speed handling. However, the best of the type were good by any standards—MG, Singer (83), Riley (96), SS100 (98), and most were entered intensively by their factories in competitions until the middle 1930s, when the big combines won control of the firms and stopped such uneconomic extravagances as racing. At the other extreme were cars such as the Wolseley Hornet Special (55), the BSA Scout (74), and the Standard Avon Special Nine (32), that (in standard form) were sports cars in name, appearance, and sound effects only.

The proliferation of cheap sports car makes during the 1930s was unprecedented, and unparalleled since. It was also an almost entirely British phenomenon, accounting for the fact that although around 100 cars from eight countries are discussed in this book, 60 per cent are British. The most notable exception was the Fiat 508S from Italy (65), which was in some respects superior to Britain's cars, having better roadholding than most, and being lighter and higher-geared. Together, these were the machines that were the direct ancestors of today's MG Midgets, Triumphs, and Hondas, and of the Fiat derivatives that swarm in Italy.

Running beside the three new types that appeared around the beginning of the decade, and continuing well into the 1930s, were the survivors of the older breeds—Lagonda (whose cars in the 1920s tradition lived on until 1937) and Frazer Nash (whose last chain-driven car was made in 1938) in Britain; and the speedsters of Auburn (66), Duesenberg (78), Cord (93), and Stutz (44) in America (the last of which was dead by 1937).

From the middle 1930s, a fourth variety of sports car developed. It was a new breed of specialized, modern competition machines, sometimes based on touring antecedents, but distinguished from its predecessors chiefly by sophistication in chassis design, which was now receiving radical attention from sports-car designers for the first time. Broadly speaking, this period saw the first general spread of the theory that a combination of very rigid frame and independent suspension was best for roadholding. Some of these cars, notably the German ones, including BMW and Adler, derived their advanced thinking from the revolutionary ideas in chassis design, first adopted in touring cars, that had taken root in Germany and Austria around 1930. Another powerful influence was the total domination of the German Mercedes-Benz and Auto-Union cars of Grand Prix racing from 1935 on in the 750-kg. formula. The two contributing factors were related, in that

advanced German–Austrian design was partly responsible for the German triumph. Grand Prix racing was now too expensive, if one was to try to compete with the state-subsidized German teams. Lack of competition for the latter meant dull races, and led to a hunt for other forms of competition, particularly among the French, who for reasons of national pride alone were anxious to provide an alternative. Most of the classic sports-car races were still in existence, but now Grands Prix for sports cars began to be added to the calendar—such were the French Grands Prix of 1936 and 1937. More interest in sports-car racing led to a spate of new competition cars, among them the Delahaye 135M (79), the Talbot-Lago (95), the Bugatti 57S and SC (94), the BMW Type 328 (75), the Adler Trumpf Sport (76), and the Alfa-Romeo 8C 2900 (101). These machines formed the advance guard of today's most sophisticated sports cars—the expensive élite ruled by Ferrari, Porsche, Aston Martin, Lotus, Ford, and the rest.

There were no British names among them: only French, German, and Italian. England in the middle and late 1930s had some new and very fine cars, but they were either out-and-out sports machines outside the cheap and nasty category, of traditional, conservative pattern—the Morgan 4/4 (84), the Squire (63), the Lagonda Rapier (57), the HRG (82)—or else they attempted to get the best of both sports and touring worlds by using big, low-stressed American engines, mildly tuned, in lighter, more roadworthy and higher-geared British chassis (72, 88, 89). The objective was maximum performance coupled with maximum reliability and flexibility, in the fast-tourer school of thought. Railton, Brough Superior, and Jensen were examples. This recipe is back in favour today. But the British cars just mentioned were in a specialized minority. The dominant characteristics of the 1930s British sports car were low price, mass-produced components, and economy of running. Together with the exotica from the Continent, they set the stage for the post-war years.

AUTHOR'S NOTES

The dates given to the cars painted are either of the particular vehicles illustrated, or, if the precise date is unknown, of the currency of the model. A reference to the descriptive text under 'The Sports Cars in Detail' (p. 109) will tell the reader which applies.

The colouring of a car as shown is not necessarily that in which it was normally seen or catalogued. It has been dictated by the exigencies of an attractive page layout. In many instances, though, cars were to be seen, if not catalogued, in almost any colour, since this could be at the discretion of the buyer (particularly in the case of chassis normally fitted with bodies supplied by outside coach-builders).

For the sake of interest and to provide an idea of the variety to be seen on the basic model shown, different body styles etc. are illustrated, even if unusual, i.e., they are not necessarily representative.

Any two views of one car are not necessarily to scale; nor are the views of different cars on the same or adjoining pages.

Approximate conversion of cylinder bore and stroke: 25.4 mm. (millimetres) = 1 inch.
Approximate conversion of engine cubic capacity: 16.4 cubic centimetres (c.c.) = 1 cubic inch.

1

Simson Supra. 1928. Germany. Water cooled, four vertical cylinders in line, 70 x 128 mm., 1950 cc. Overhead valves operated by two overhead camshafts. Four valves per cylinder. Four forward speeds. Half-elliptic springs, underslung at rear.

2

Austro-Daimler ADM III. 1928. Austria. Water cooled, six vertical cylinders in line, 76 x 100 mm., 2994 cc. Overhead valves operated by single shaft-driven overhead camshaft. Four forward speeds. Half-elliptic front springs, cantilever rear springs.

3

Stutz Black Hawk. 1928. U.S.A. Water cooled, eight vertical cylinders in line, 82 x 115 mm., 4735 cc. Overhead valves operated by single chain-driven overhead camshaft. Four forward speeds. Half-elliptic springs front and rear, underslung at rear.

4

Amilcar CGSs. 1928. France. Water cooled, four vertical cylinders in line, 60 x 95 mm., 1074 cc. Side valves. Three or four forward speeds. Half-elliptic springs at front, quarter-elliptic springs at rear.

5

Th. Schneider. 1928. France. Water cooled, four vertical cylinders in line, 72 x 120 mm., 1954 cc. Pushrod-operated overhead valves. Four forward speeds. Half-elliptic springs front and rear.

6

Sara. 1928. France. Air cooled, six vertical cylinders in line, 66 x 88 mm., 1806 cc.
Pushrod-operated overhead valves. Four forward speeds. Half-elliptic front springs,
quarter-elliptic rear springs.

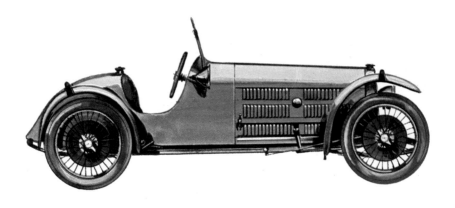

7

Lombard AL3. 1928. France. Water cooled, four vertical cylinders in line, 61.5 x 92 mm., 1083 cc. Overhead valves operated by two overhead camshafts. Optional Cozette supercharger. Four forward speeds. Half-elliptic springs front and rear.

8

D'Yrsan. 1928. France. Water cooled, four vertical cylinders in line, 62 x 90 mm.,
1088 cc. Pushrod-operated overhead valves. Cozette supercharger. Four forward
speeds. At front half elliptic springs or independent front suspension by two transverse superimposed springs, at rear quarter-elliptic springs.

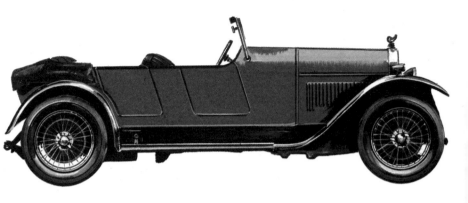

9

Delage DIS. 1928. France. Water cooled, four vertical cylinders in line, 75 x 120 mm., 2120 cc. Pushrod-operated overhead valves. Four forward speeds. Half-elliptic springs front and rear.

10

Bugatti Type 43. 1928. France. Water cooled, eight vertical cylinders in line, 60 x 100 mm., 2261 cc. Overhead valves operated by single overhead camshaft. Two inlet and one exhaust valve per cylinder. Four forward speeds. Half-elliptic front suspension, reversed quarter-elliptic rear suspension.

11
Rally Type ABC. 1928. France. Water cooled, four vertical cylinders in line, 59 x 100 mm., 1094 cc. Pushrod-operated overhead valves. Four forward speeds. Half-elliptic springs front and rear.

12

M.G. 14/40. 1928. Great Britain. Water cooled, four vertical cylinders in line, 75 x 102 mm., 1802 cc. Side valves. Four forward speeds. Half-elliptic springs front and rear.

13

Austin Seven Super Sports and Ulster. 1928-32. Great Britain. Water cooled, four vertical cylinders in line, 56 x 76 mm., 747 cc. Side valves. Cozette supercharger optional. Three forward speeds. Single transverse front spring, quarter-elliptic rear springs.

14

O.M. Type 665 Superba. 1928. Italy. Water cooled, six vertical cylinders in line, 69 x 100 mm., 1991 cc. Side valves. Four forward speeds. Half-elliptic springs front and rear.

15

Italo Tipo 65S. 1928. Italy. Water cooled, six vertical cylinders in line, 65 x 100 mm., 1991 cc. Overhead valves operated by two overhead camshafts. Four forward speeds. Half-elliptic springs front and rear.

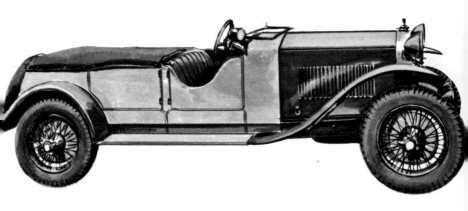

16

Fiat Tipo 509S. 1928. Italy. Water cooled, four vertical cylinders in line, 57 x 97 mm., 990 cc. Overhead valves operated by single chain driven overhead camshaft. Three forward speeds. Half-elliptic springs front and rear, underslung at rear.

17

Mercedes-Benz SSK. 1929. Germany. Water cooled, six vertical cylinders in line, 100 x 150 mm., 7010 cc. Roots-type supercharger. Overhead valves operated by single overhead camshaft. Four forward speeds. Half-elliptic suspension front and rear.

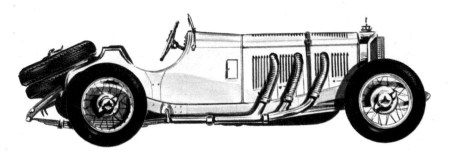

AUSTRO-DAIMLER ADR SPORT

18

Austro-Daimler ADR Sport. 1929. Austria. Water cooled, six vertical cylinders in line, 76 x 110 mm., 2994 cc. Overhead valves operated by single overhead camshaft. Four forward speeds. Half-elliptic front suspension, independent rear suspension by swing axles and transverse spring. Tubular backbone chassis.

AUSTRO-DAIMLER ADR6 BERGMEISTER

19

Austro-Daimler ADR6 Bergmeister. 1933. Austria. Water cooled, six vertical cylinders in line, 82 x 115 mm., 3614 cc. Overhead valves operated by overhead camshaft. Four forward speeds. Half-elliptic front suspension, independent rear suspension by swing axles and transverse spring. Tubular backbone chassis.

20

DuPont Model G Le Mans Speedster. 1929. U.S.A. Water cooled, eight vertical cylinders in line, 85 x 114 mm., 5180 cc. Side valves. Four forward speeds. Half-elliptic springs front and rear.

CORD L29

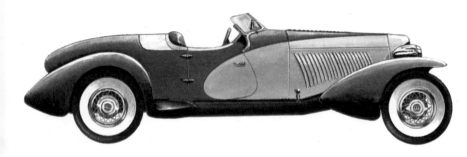

21

Cord L29. 1929. U.S.A. Water cooled, eight vertical cylinders in line, 82.5 x 114 mm., 4800 cc. Front wheel drive. Side valves. Three forward speeds. Front suspension by four quarter-elliptic springs, rear suspension half-elliptic springs.

22

Tracta. 1929-30. France. Water cooled, four vertical cylinders in line, 70 x 105 mm., 1614 cc. Front wheel drive. Pushrod-operated overhead valves. Four forward speeds. Independent front suspension by transverse leaf spring, rear suspension by inverted quarter-elliptic springs.

23

Ariès 3-Litre Sport. 1929. France. Water cooled, four vertical cylinders in line, 82 x 140 mm., 2952 cc. Overhead valves operated by single overhead camshaft. Four forward speeds. Half-elliptic springs front and rear.

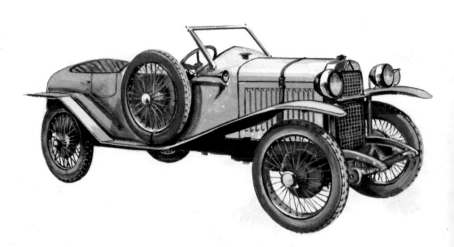

24

Bentley 4½-Litre. 1929. Great Britain. Water cooled, four vertical cylinders in line,
100 x 140 mm., 4398 cc. Overhead valves operated by single overhead camshaft.
Four forward speeds. Half-elliptic springs front and rear.

25

Bentley Speed Six. 1929-30. Great Britain. Water cooled, six vertical cylinders in line, 100 x 140 mm., 6597 cc. Overhead valves operated by single overhead camshaft. Four forward speeds. Half-elliptic springs front and rear.

26

H.E. Six. 1929. Great Britain. Water cooled, four vertical cylinders in line, 65 x 115 mm., 2290 cc. Side valves. Four forward speeds. Half-elliptic springs front and rear.

RILEY BROOKLANDS

27

Riley Brooklands. 1929. Great Britain. Water cooled, four vertical cylinders in line, 60.3 x 95.2 mm., 1087 cc. Overhead valves operated by two high camshafts. Four forward speeds. Half-elliptic springs front and rear.

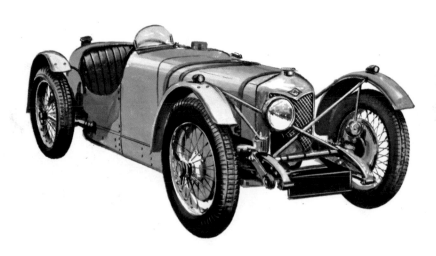

28

Lea-Francis Hyper Sports. 1929. Great Britain. Water cooled, four vertical cylinders in line, 69 x 100 mm., 1496 cc. Cozette supercharger. Pushrod-operated overhead valves. Four forward speeds. Half-elliptic springs front and rear.

29

Alvis Front-Wheel Drive. 1929. Great Britain. Water cooled, four vertical cylinders in line, 68 x 102 mm., 1482 cc. Overhead valves operated by single overhead camshaft. Four forward speeds. Independent suspension by eight quarter-elliptic springs at the front, by quarter-elliptic springs and torque arms at the rear.

MORGAN AERO

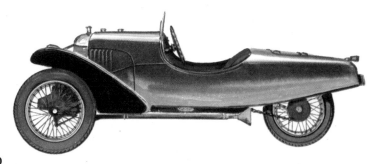

30

Morgan Aero. 1929. Great Britain. Water cooled, two cylinders in vee formation, 85.7 x 95 mm., 1096 cc. Pushrod-operated overhead valves. Two forward speeds. Dog clutches actuating chain final drive. Independent front suspension by sliding pillars and coil springs, quarter-elliptic rear suspension.

MORGAN SUPER SPORTS

31

Morgan Super Sports. 1934. Great Britain. Air or water-cooled, two cylinders in vee formation, 85.5 x 85.5 mm., 990 cc. Pushrod-operated overhead valves or side valves. Plate clutch. Three forward speeds. Single chain final drive. Independent front suspension by sliding pillars and coil springs, quarter-elliptic rear suspension.

STANDARD AVON SPECIAL

32

Standard Avon Special. 1929. Great Britain. Water cooled, four vertical cylinders in line, 63.5 x 102 mm., 1287 cc. Side valves. Three forward speeds. Underslung worm final drive. Half-elliptic springs front and rear.

ROLLS-ROYCE PHANTOM I CONTINENTAL

33

Rolls-Royce Phantom I Continental. 1929. Great Britain. Water cooled, six vertical cylinders in line, 108 x 140 mm., 7668 cc. Pushrod-operated overhead valves. Four forward speeds. Half-elliptic front springs, cantilever rear springs.

ROLLS-ROYCE PHANTOM II CONTINENTAL

34

Rolls-Royce Phantom II Continental. 1933. Great Britain. Water cooled, six vertical cylinders in line, 108 x 140 mm., 7668 cc. Pushrod-operated overhead valves. Four forward speeds. Half-elliptic springs front and rear.

35

Fiat Tipo 525S, 525SS. 1929, 1930. Italy. Water cooled, six vertical cylinders in line, 82 x 118 mm., 3740 cc. Side valves. Four forward speeds. Half-elliptic springs front and rear.

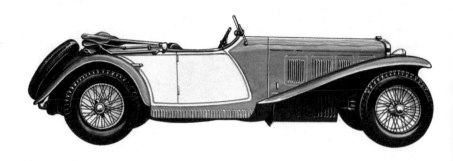

36

Minerva AKS. 1929. Belgium. Water cooled, six vertical cylinders in line, 95 x 140 mm., 4954 cc. Knight-type double sleeve valves. Four forward speeds. Half-elliptic springs front and rear.

JORDAN SPEEDWAY EIGHT

37

Jordan Speedway Eight. 1930. U.S.A. Water cooled, eight vertical cylinders in line, 85 x 114 mm., 5180 cc. Side valves. Four forward speeds. Half-elliptic springs front and rear.

38

M.G. 18/100 Tigress. 1930. Great Britain. Water cooled, six vertical cylinders in line, 69 x 100 mm., 2468 cc. Overhead valves operated by single overhead camshaft. Four forward speeds. Half-elliptic springs front and rear.

39

M.G. M Midget, Double Twelve Midget. 1930. Great Britain. Water cooled, four vertical cylinders in line, 57 x 83 mm., 847 cc. Overhead valves operated by a single overhead camshaft. Three forward speeds. Half-elliptic springs front and rear.

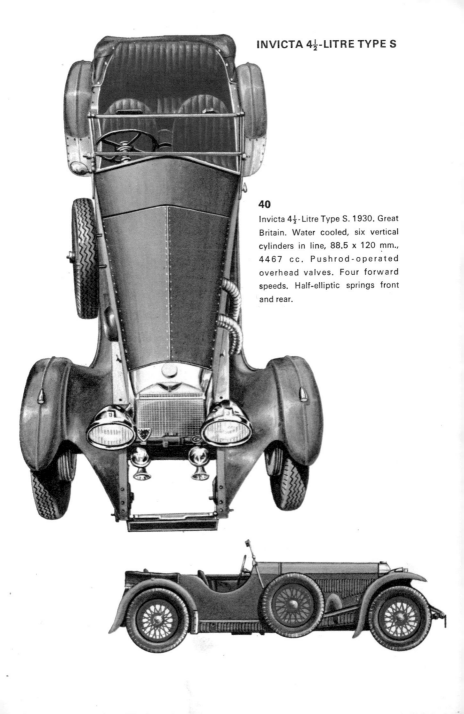

INVICTA 4½-LITRE TYPE S

40

Invicta 4½-Litre Type S. 1930. Great Britain. Water cooled, six vertical cylinders in line, 88.5 x 120 mm., 4467 cc. Pushrod-operated overhead valves. Four forward speeds. Half-elliptic springs front and rear.

41

O.M. 2.2-Litre. 1930. Italy. Water cooled, six vertical cylinders in line, 67 x 100 mm., 2243 cc. Side valves. Four forward speeds. Half-elliptic springs front and rear.

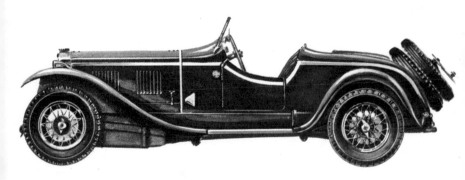

42

Alfa-Romeo 6C 1750GS. 1930, 1933. Italy. Water cooled, six vertical cylinders in line, 65 x 88 mm., 1752 cc. Overhead valves operated by two overhead camshafts. Roots-type supercharger. Four forward speeds. Half-elliptic springs front and rear.

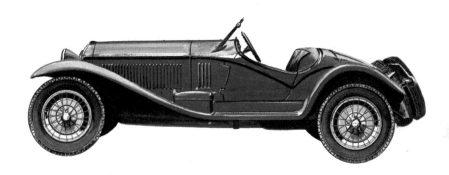

43

Mercedes-Benz 370S Mannheim Sport. 1931. Germany. Water cooled, six vertical cylinders in line, 82.5 x 115 mm., 3663 cc. Side valves. Four forward speeds. Half-elliptic suspension front and rear.

44

Stutz DV32 Bearcat. 1931-35. U.S.A. Water cooled, eight vertical cylinders in line, 85 x 114 mm., 5270 cc. Overhead valves operated by two overhead camshafts. Four valves per cylinder. Four forward speeds. Half-elliptic springs front and rear.

DELAGE D8SS

45

Delage D8SS. 1931-35. France. Water cooled, eight vertical cylinders in line, 77 x 109 mm., 4050 cc. Pushrod-operated overhead valves. Four forward speeds. Half-elliptic springs front and rear.

46

Derby L2 6CV. 1931-34. France. Water cooled, four vertical cylinders in line,
60 x 97 mm., 1100 cc. Front wheel drive. Pushrod operated overhead valves. Four
forward speeds. Independent suspension front and rear by forked pivoted arms and
transverse leaf springs.

DERBY 1500

47

Derby 1500. 1931-34. France. Water cooled, four vertical cylinders in line, 69 x 100
mm., 1496 cc. Front wheel drive. Pushrod operated overhead valves. Four forward
speeds. Independent suspension front and rear by forked pivoted arms and transverse leaf springs.

48

Alvis 12/60. 1931-32. Great Britain. Water cooled, four vertical cylinders in line, 69 x 110 mm., 1645 cc. Pushrod-operated overhead valves. Four forward speeds. Half-elliptic springs front and rear.

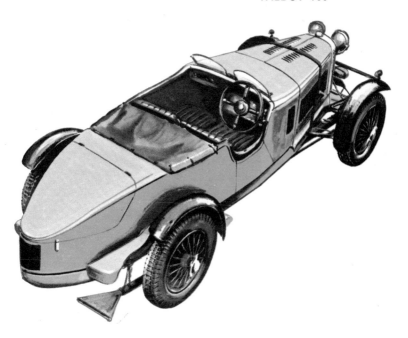

49

Talbot 105. 1931-37. Great Britain. Water cooled, six vertical cylinders in line,
75 x 112 mm., 2969 cc. Pushrod-operated overhead valves. Four forward speeds.
Half-elliptic front springs, quarter-elliptic rear springs.

MASERATI 8C-1100

50

Maserati 8C-1100. 1931. Italy. Water cooled, eight vertical cylinders in line, 51 x 66 mm., 1078 cc. Roots supercharger. Overhead valves operated by two overhead camshafts. Four forward speeds. Half-elliptic springs front and rear.

51

Alfa-Romeo 8C 2300 Monza. 1931-33. Italy. Water cooled, eight cylinders in line, 65 x 88 mm., 2336 cc. Overhead valves operated by two overhead camshafts. Roots-type supercharger. Four forward speeds. Half-elliptic springs front and rear.

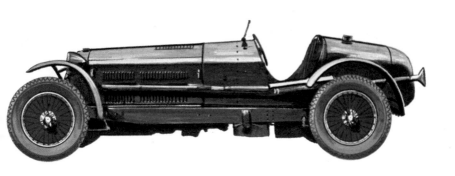

52

Bugatti Type 55. 1932. France. Water cooled, eight vertical cylinders in line, 60 x 100 mm., 2270 cc. Overhead valves operated by two overhead camshafts. Four forward speeds.

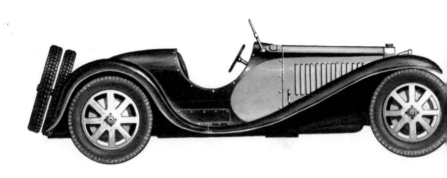

53

Lagonda Two Litre. 1928-32. Great Britain. Water cooled, four cylinders in line, 72 x 120 mm., 1954 cc. Overhead valves operated by two high camshafts. Four forward speeds. Half-elliptic springs front and rear.

ALVIS SA SPEED TWENTY

54

Alvis SA Speed Twenty. 1932-33. Great Britain. Water cooled, six vertical cylinders in line, 73 x 100 mm., 2511 cc. Pushrod-operated overhead valves. Four forward speeds. Half-elliptic springs front and rear.

55

Wolseley Hornet Special. 1932-33. Great Britain. Water cooled, six vertical cylinders in line, 57 x 83 mm., 1271 cc. Overhead valves operated by single overhead camshaft. Four forward speeds. Half-elliptic springs front and rear.

ASTON MARTIN LE MANS

56

Aston Martin Le Mans. 1933-34. Great Britain. Water cooled, four vertical cylinders in line, 69 x 99 mm., 1495 cc. Overhead valves operated by single overhead camshaft. Four forward speeds. Half-elliptic springs front and rear.

57

Lagonda Rapier. 1933-36. Great Britain. Water cooled, four vertical cylinders in line, 62.5 x 90 mm., 1104 cc. Overhead valves operated by two overhead camshafts. Four forward speeds. Half-elliptic springs front and rear.

58

M.G. J2 Midget. 1933. Great Britain. Water cooled, four vertical cylinders in line, 57 x 83 mm., 847 cc. Overhead valves operated by a single overhead camshaft. Four forward speeds. Half-elliptic springs front and rear.

59

M.G. L Magna. 1933. Great Britain. Water cooled, six cylinders in line, 57 x 71 mm., 1087 cc. Overhead valves operated by a single overhead camshaft. Four forward speeds. Half-elliptic springs front and rear.

60

M.G. K3 Magnette. 1933-34. Great Britain. Water cooled, six vertical cylinders in line, 57 x 71 mm., 1087 cc., supercharged. Overhead valves operated by single overhead camshaft. Four forward speeds, Wilson preselector or normal gearbox. Half-elliptic springs front and rear.

61

Vale Special. 1933-36. Great Britain. Water cooled, four vertical cylinders in line 56.5 x 83 mm., 832 cc. Side valves. Four forward speeds. Half-elliptic suspension front and rear.

62

Wikov Sport. 1933. Czechoslovakia. Water cooled, four vertical cylinders in line, 66 x 108 mm., 1480 cc. Overhead valves operated by single overhead camshaft. Four forward speeds. Half-elliptic front springs, quarter elliptic rear springs.

63

Squire. 1934-36. Great Britain. Water cooled, four vertical cylinders in line, 69 x 100 mm., 1496 cc. Roots-type supercharger. Overhead valves operated by two overhead camshafts. Wilson preselector gearbox. Four forward speeds. Half-elliptic springs front and rear.

BENTLEY 3½-LITRE

64

Bentley 3½-Litre. 1934. Great Britain. Water cooled, six vertical cylinders in line, 82.5 x 114 mm., 3669 cc. Pushrod-operated overhead valves. Four forward speeds. Half-elliptic springs front and rear.

65

Fiat Tipo 508S. 1934, 1935. Italy. Water cooled, four vertical cylinders in line, 65 x 75 mm., 995 cc. First series: side valves. Second series: pushrod-operated overhead valves. First series: three forward speeds. Second series: four forward speeds. Half-elliptic springs front and rear.

66

Auburn Model 851 Speedster. 1935. U.S.A. Water cooled, eight vertical cylinders in line, 78 x 120 mm., 4600 cc. Centrifugal supercharger. Side valves. Three forward speeds, Columbia two-speed axle. Half-elliptic springs front and rear.

67

Frazer Nash T.T. Replica. 1935. Great Britain. Water cooled, four vertical cylinders in line, 69 x 100 mm., 1496 cc. Overhead valves operated by single overhead camshaft. Four forward speeds. Quarter-elliptic springs front and rear.

RILEY IMP

68

Riley Imp. 1935. Great Britain. Water cooled, four vertical cylinders in line, 60.3 x 95.2 mm., 1087 cc. Overhead valves operated by two high camshafts. Four forward speeds. Half-elliptic springs front and rear.

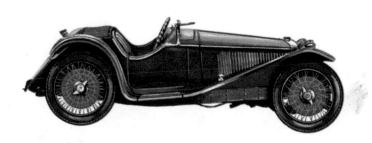

69

Triumph Gloria Southern Cross. 1935. Great Britain. Water cooled, four vertical cylinders in line, 66 x 90 mm., 1232 cc. Overhead inlet, side exhaust valves. Four forward speeds. Half-elliptic springs front and rear.

MARENDAZ SPECIAL 15/98 H.P.

70
Marendaz Special 15/98 h.p. 1935-36. Great Britain. Water cooled, six vertical cylinders in line, 65 x 100 mm., 1991 cc. Overhead inlet, side exhaust valves. Four forward speeds. Half-elliptic front suspension, cantilever rear suspension.

71
Austin Seven Nippy, 1934-38, and Speedy, 1934-35. Great Britain. Water cooled,
four vertical cylinders in line, 56 x 76 mm., 747 cc. Side valves. Four forward speeds.
Front suspension by transverse leaf spring, quarter-elliptic rear suspension.

RAILTON LIGHT SPORTS TOURER

72

Railton Light Sports Tourer. 1935-36. Great Britain. Water cooled, eight vertical cylinders in line, 76 x 114 mm., 4168 cc. Side valves. Three forward speeds. Half-elliptic springs front and rear.

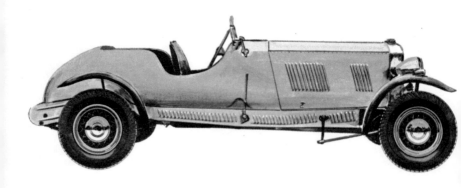

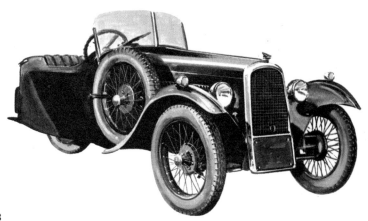

73

B.S.A. Three-Wheeler. 1935. Great Britain. Air cooled, two cylinders in vee formation, 85 x 90 mm., 1021 cc. Front wheel drive. Side valves. Three forward speeds. Independent front suspension by four transverse quarter-elliptic springs, rear suspension by leaf spring and hinged arm.

B.S.A. SCOUT

74

B.S.A. Scout, 1936-39. Great Britain. Water cooled, four vertical cylinders in line, 63.5 x 95 mm., 1204 cc. Front wheel drive. Side valves. Three forward speeds. Underslung worm final drive. Independent front suspension by four transverse quarter-elliptic springs, half-elliptic rear suspension.

75

BMW Type 328. 1936-40, 1939-40. Germany. Water cooled, six vertical cylinders in line, 66 x 96 mm., 1971 cc. Overhead valves operated by vertical pushrods and rockers (inlets) and transverse pushrods and rockers (exhaust). Four forward speeds. Independent front suspension by wishbones and transverse leaf spring. Rear half-elliptic springs.

ADLER TRUMPF SPORT

76

Adler Trumpf Sport. 1936-38. Germany. Water cooled, four vertical cylinders in line, 74.25 x 95 mm., 1645 cc. Side valves. Front wheel drive. Four forward speeds. Independent front suspension by transverse leaf springs, independent rear suspension by trailing arms and cantilever springs.

ADLER TRUMPF JUNIOR SPORT

77

Adler Trumpf Junior Sport. 1936. Germany. Water cooled, four vertical cylinders in line, 65 x 75 mm., 995 cc. Side valves. Front wheel drive. Four forward speeds. Independent front suspension by transverse leaf springs, independent rear suspension by leading arms and torsion bars.

78

Duesenberg SJ Speedster. 1936. U.S.A. Water cooled, eight vertical cylinders in line, 95 x 121 mm., 6882 cc. Overhead valves operated by two overhead camshafts. Four valves per cylinder. Three forward speeds. Half-elliptic springs front and rear.

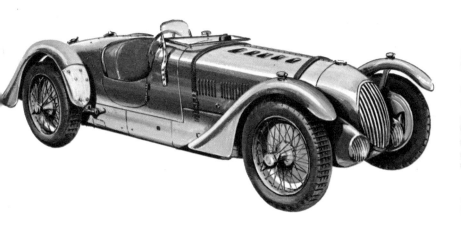

79

Delahaye Type 135M Competition. 1936-39. France. Water cooled, six vertical cylinders in line, 84 x 107 mm., 3557 cc. Pushrod-operated overhead valves. Four forward speeds. Manual or Cotal electric gearbox. Independent front suspension by radius arms and transverse leaf spring, half-elliptic rear suspension.

HOTCHKISS GRAND SPORT

80

Hotchkiss Grand Sport. 1936. France. Water cooled, six vertical cylinders in line. 86 x 100 mm., 3485 cc. Pushrod-operated overhead valves. Four forward speeds, Half-elliptic springs front and rear.

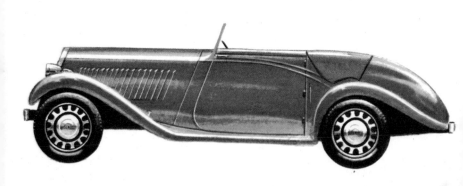

81

Aston Martin Speed Model. 1936-38. Great Britain. Water cooled, four vertical cylinders in line, 78 x 102 mm., 1950 cc. Overhead valves operated by single overhead camshaft. Four forward speeds. Half-elliptic springs front and rear.

82

HRG. 1936-38. Great Britain. Water cooled, four vertical cylinders in line, 69 x 100 mm., 1496 cc. (Meadows engine) or 60 x 95 mm., 1074 cc. (Singer engine). Pushrod-operated overhead valves (Meadows) or single overhead camshaft (Singer). Four forward speeds. Quarter-elliptic front suspension, half-elliptic rear suspension.

83

Singer Le Mans Replica. 1936. Great Britain. Water cooled, four vertical cylinders in line, 60 x 86 mm., 972 cc. Overhead valves operated by single overhead camshaft Four forward speeds. Half-elliptic springs front and rear.

MORGAN 4/4

84

Morgan 4/4. 1936-39. Great Britain. Water cooled, four vertical cylinders in line,
63 x 90 mm., 1122 cc. Pushrod-operated overhead inlet valves, side exhaust valves.
Four forward speeds. Independent front suspension by sliding pillars and coil
springs, half-elliptic rear springs.

85

M.G. TA Midget. 1936-39. Great Britain. Water cooled, four vertical cylinders in line, 63.5 x 102 mm., 1292 cc. Pushrod-operated overhead valves. Four forward speeds. Half-elliptic springs front and rear.

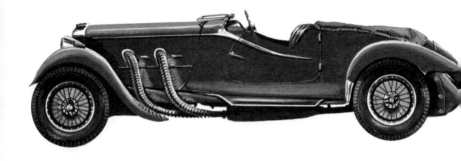

86

Lagonda Rapide. 1936-37. Great Britain. Water cooled, six cylinders in line, 88.5 x 120.6 mm., 4453 cc. Pushrod-operated overhead valves. Four forward speeds. Half-elliptic springs front and rear.

87

AC 16/80. 1936. Great Britain. Water cooled, six vertical cylinders in line, 65 x 100 mm., 1991 cc. Overhead valves operated by single overhead camshaft. Wilson preselector or manual gearbox. Four forward speeds. Half-elliptic springs front and rear.

JENSEN S-TYPE

88

Jensen S-type. 1937. Great Britain. Water cooled, eight cylinders in vee formation, 78 x 95 mm., 3622 cc. Side valves. Three forward speeds, two-speed axle. Transverse spring and radius arm suspension front and rear.

89

Brough Superior. 1936-40. Great Britain. Water cooled, six vertical cylinders in line, 76.2 x 127 mm., 3435 cc. Side valves. Three forward speeds. Half-elliptic springs front and rear.

MERCEDES-BENZ 540K

90

Mercedes-Benz 540K. 1937-39. Germany. Water cooled, six vertical cylinders in line, 88 x 111 mm., 5401 cc., supercharged. Pushrod-operated overhead valves. Four forward speeds and overdrive. Independent suspension by parallel wishbones and coil springs at the front, by swing axles and coil springs at the rear.

91

Hansa 1700 and 1700 Sport. 1937. Germany. Water cooled, six vertical cylinders in line, 65 x 82 mm., 1640 cc. Pushrod-operated overhead valves. Four forward speeds. Independent suspension by double transverse springs at front, swing-axles and transverse leaf spring at rear.

92

BMW Type 319/1. 1937. Germany. Water cooled, six vertical cylinders in line, 65 x 96 mm., 1911 cc. Pushrod-operated overhead valves. Four forward speeds. Independent front suspension by wishbones and transverse leaf spring, rear half-elliptic springs.

93

Cord 812. 1937. U.S.A. Water cooled, eight cylinders in vee formation, 89 x 95 mm., 4730 cc. Supercharged. Front wheel drive. Side valves. Four forward speeds. Independent front suspension by trailing arms and transverse spring, rear suspension half elliptic.

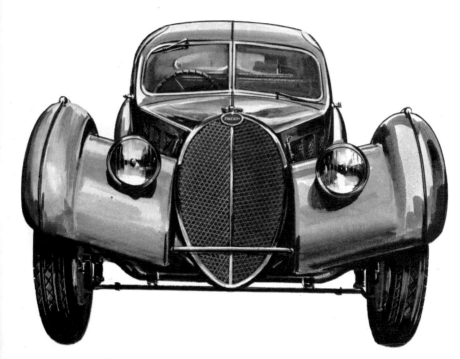

94

Bugatti Type 57SC. 1937-38. France. Water cooled, eight vertical cylinders in line, 72 x 100 mm., 3250 cc. Overhead valves operated by two overhead camshafts. Four forward speeds. Half-elliptic front suspension, reversed quarter-elliptic rear suspension.

95

Talbot-Lago. 1937. France. Water cooled, six vertical cylinders in line, 90 x 104.5 mm., 3996 cc. Pushrod-operated overhead valves. Four forward speeds. Wilson preselector gearbox. Independent front suspension by wishbones and transverse leaf spring. Half-elliptic rear suspension.

RILEY SPRITE

96

Riley Sprite. 1937. Great Britain. Water cooled, four vertical cylinders in line, 69 x 100 mm., 1496 cc. Overhead valves operated by two high camshafts. Four forward speeds. Half-elliptic springs front and rear.

97

Alta Two Litre. 1938-39. Great Britain. Water cooled, four vertical cylinders in line, 79 x 100 mm., 1960 cc. Supercharged. Overhead valves operated by two overhead camshafts. Four forward speeds. Front half-elliptic springs, quarter-elliptic rear springs.

98

SS100. 1938, 1939. Great Britain. Water cooled, six vertical cylinders in line, 73 x 106 mm., 2664 cc. (2½ Litre) ; 82 x 110 mm., 3485 cc. (3½ Litre). Pushrod-operated overhead valves. Four forward speeds. Half-elliptic springs front and rear.

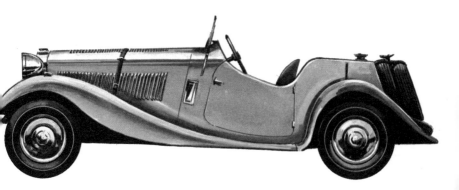

99

British Salmson 20/90. 1938. Great Britain. Water cooled, six vertical cylinders in line. 75 x 98 mm., 2590 cc. Overhead valves operated by two overhead camshafts. Four forward speeds. Independent front suspension by transverse leaf springs, quarter-elliptic rear suspension.

ATLANTA 1½-LITRE

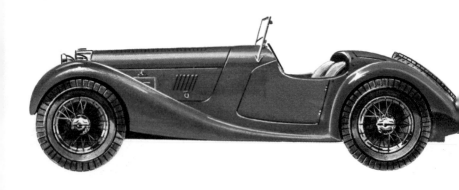

100

Atalanta 1½ Litre. 1938. Great Britain. Water cooled, four vertical cylinders in line, 69 x 100 mm., 1496 cc. Overhead valves operated by single overhead camshaft. Three valves per cylinder. Four forward speeds. Independent suspension by double coil springs and trailing links at front, swing axles at rear.

101

Alfa-Romeo 8C 2900B. 1938. Italy. Water cooled, eight cylinders in line, 68 x 100 mm., 2905 cc. Overhead valves operated by two overhead camshafts. Twin Roots-type superchargers. Four forward speeds. Independent front suspension by trailing links and coil springs. Independent rear suspension by swing axles and transverse leaf spring.

RAYMOND MAYS

102

Raymond Mays. 1939. Great Britain. Water cooled, eight cylinders in vee formation, 63.5 x 106 mm., 2686 cc. Side valves. Four forward speeds. Independent front suspension by transverse spring and wishbones, half-elliptic rear suspension.

THE SPORTS CARS IN DETAIL

1 SIMSON SUPRA, 1928, Germany

The Simson emanated from a firm of arms manufacturers, and had done since 1911, but not until the 1920s did it make any mark. It then did so in no uncertain fashion, being (by then) a predominantly sporting car made by one of the very few German car manufacturers to specialize in such machinery and survive in the grim, austerity-ridden post-war Reich, which lacked the export markets that liked sports cars. The firm's new image dated from the 1924 Berlin Show, when the S-type Simson or Simson Supra was announced. It was intended as a limited-production car selling at a high price to the discerning market that bought Bugattis (10), and appreciated quality, elegance, and modern design. Paul Henze was the designer; indeed, his new machine showed much of the influence of another of his designs, the Steiger sports car. The long-stroke engine had four cylinders with four valves per cylinder operated by two shaft-driven overhead camshafts. There was a roller-bearing crankshaft, and dry-sump lubrication. Twin carburettors were fitted, and on the exhaust side, there was one pipe per cylinder. Power output was a conserva-. tive-sounding 60 b.h.p. at 4000 r.p.m. The gear-box enjoyed four close ratios. There were brakes on all four wheels, on Belgian Adex patents. The centre of gravity was low, and weight distribution good, so this car handled well, as it needed to, with an 85 m.p.h. maximum. Only thirty were built in all. Alongside them, there was built the Type SO, to a total of 750 units. It was more 'touring', but it was still a far cry from the average pedestrian offerings of German manufacturers of the time (1924-8). Into a longer chassis was installed a single-carburettor engine without separate downpipes to each cylinder, and with one overhead camshaft and two valves per cylinder only.

2 AUSTRO-DAIMLER ADMIII, 1928, Austria

Just before Ferdinand Porsche left Vienna to return to Daimler, he designed a fine fast tourer for Austro-Daimler; the Type ADMI of 1923. It was then a very modern, sophisticated machine, with its overhead-camshaft engine with aluminium cylinders and cast-iron detachable liners (in pursuance of aviation practice, which was followed by the most advanced luxury cars of the day), and unit construction of engine, radiator, steering-box, and gear-box. There were front wheel brakes. Rated at 10/50 P.S., its six-cylinder engine was just over $2\frac{1}{2}$ litres in size. The car was the first Austro-Daimler to bear the attractive, pear-shaped radiator that all were to carry till the end; until then, a sharp and aggressive vee radiator in the German fashion had been worn. The indicated power of 50 b.h.p. was developed at 2800 r.p.m., and sufficed for a 60 m.p.h. maximum speed. In 1925 this touring car was supplemented by the ADMII, a sports version with two carburettors, 60 b.h.p. at 3100 r.p.m., and (in its hottest Alpine-sports form) 85 m.p.h.

These cars were based on those that won the 1924 Austrian Alpine Trials outright. The engine was enlarged to 3 litres in 1926, by increasing the bore. This unit powered the ultimate development of the ADM range, the ADMIII. This was to be had in 11/70 P.S. or normal form, when over 80 m.p.h. was available, and as the 11/100 P.S. with short chassis, 100 b.h.p. at 4000 r.p.m., and 100 m.p.h. By now the cantilever rear suspension was looking very out of place, being usually seen on pure touring machinery; but the handling, the very large brakes, and the steering were all excellent. The ADMIII won the team prize in the 1928 Ulster Tourist Trophy Race. In 1929 it gave way to Karl Rabe's still more up to date ADR series (18), with tubular backbone frame and independent rear suspension.

3 STUTZ BLACK HAWK, 1928, U.S.A.

The last cars of the Stutz régime that had produced the famous Bearcat, America's most renowned sports car, were made in 1925, and with them died the last traces of Harry C. Stutz on the car that bore his name. The popularity of speedsters, with which Stutz were always associated, was on the wane. The new rule of Frederick E. Moskovics brought ultra-modern influences. Moskovics, a salesman and engineer, ex-Marmon and Franklin, gave the public beauty, safety, and comfort; all cloaking high mechanical efficiency that made his new Vertical-Eight Stutz a fast car. The Model AA of 1926, designed by C. R. Greuter

and Paul Bastien, combined overhead-camshaft operation of the valves (directly actuated) with the silence and refinement associated with far less powerful, more agricultural machinery. The crankshaft had nine bearings, and was fully balanced. The underslung worm final drive made for low build as well as quietness, and the fine Brewster bodies completed the effect of handsomeness. The low centre of gravity and very rigid chassis afforded good roadholding. Hydraulic brakes were fitted from the start, even if the Timken hydrostatic system at first supplied was not notably efficient. There was centralized chassis lubrication. The Vertical-Eight's performance, though deliberately subordinated to tamer qualities, was well above average, since the 4·7-litre engine produced 92 b.h.p. at 3200 r.p.m.—Packard and Lincoln, other high performers, gave less power from more capacity. Power rose to 95 b.h.p. in 1927. Maximum speed was between 75 and 80 m.p.h., and 10–50 m.p.h. in top gear occupied a mere 15 seconds. A variety of gear ratios from 3·6 : 1 to 5·5 : 1 was available. In all major respects, the new Stutz was an utterly untypical American car, yet such was its excellence, immediately recognized, that the 1926 sales were five times those for 1925.

The Model BB of 1928 brought many improvements. An engine with slightly larger bore gave 115 b.h.p., but the main gain was in the Lockheed hydraulic brakes; later servo assisted. The Black Hawk Speedsters on the BB chassis (see illustrations), were formidable machines. Their two- or four-passenger bodies were designed with the help of Frank Lockhart. They could be had with high-compression 125-b.h.p. engines and 3 : 1 axle ratios, giving a maximum speed of over 85 m.p.h. in normal form. Moskovics took a strong and consistent interest in competitions, making the Stutz the most formidable American contender at home and abroad. In 1927 Glen Shultz's Special with independent rear suspension made fastest time at the Pike's Peak hill-climb. Stutz set a new transcontinental record, and won the first Atlantic City stock-car race. Both glory and defeat were to come in 1928. A Black Hawk Speedster came within an ace of winning the Le Mans 24-hour Race, finishing second after a long and close struggle with the leading Bentley. W. O. Bentley himself admitted that the Stutz cornered better than his cars. These Le Mans cars were capable of 95 m.p.h., but were hampered by their three-speed gear-boxes. Unfortunately, Frank Lockhart was killed in the beautiful twin-supercharged, Miller-engined Stutz record car that year, and a normal Stutz lost its famous contest with the much bigger and more powerful (8 litres, 220 b.h.p.) Hispano-Suiza Boulogne at Indianapolis. However, the contest had a beneficial outcome for Stutz indirectly. Charles T. Weymann, whose Hispano-Suiza had been victorious, was so impressed with the Stutz that he backed the make's Le Mans entry which was so nearly successful. One driver was Robert Bloch, who had shared the wheel of the Hispano-Suiza at Indianapolis. The cars were fitted with Weymann fabric bodies, and in the same year Stutz became the pioneer of this type of body construction in America; a strengthen-

ing of its 'European' image. The Stutz Special again made best time at the Pike's Peak hill-climb—and again in 1929 and 1930. Later it was given a DV32 engine (44). The 1928 version was supercharged. A Roots-type super-charger was fitted to the three cars entered for Le Mans in 1929, though they ran unblown in the event. Power output supercharged was up to 155 b.h.p. at 3800 r.p.m., which made these genuine 100 m.p.h. cars. They had four-speed gear-boxes. They only managed fifth place, but were the only American competitors to live with the Speed Six Bentleys. To legalize the entry, twenty-five supercharged cars were built that year. By this time, the Model BB had been superseded by the Model M, current until 1931, which had a larger bore, 5·3 litres and a top speed of nearly 100 m.p.h., though the big improvement was the provision of a four-speed gear-box on the normal touring car. This was dropped in 1932 in deference to popular demand, and the three-speed Vertical-Eights were sold until around 1935. In their last years, the Eights were overshadowed by the glamorous DV32 (44).

4 AMILCAR CGSs, 1928, France

In 1920 the Amilcar was just one of a host of new sporting *voiturettes* for the modest man that had appeared or were appearing like a rash from back-street workshops in Paris and its suburbs. This Type CC differed from its competitors mainly in respect of being made very largely in its own factory, instead of being simply assembled there from proprietary parts, and in having (and adhering to) a side-valve engine. There were quarter-elliptic springs all round, no differential, and unit construction of engine and three-speed gear-box. The CS was a more sporting version still, with a larger (985 c.c.) engine and 23 b.h.p. instead of 18. With a win in the 1922 Bol d'Or Race, the make began to build up the image of a successful competition car. The works racing machines of 1924 had an engine enlarged to 1074 c.c., and were the basis of the Type CGS production car of the same year. This had front-wheel brakes for the first time, half-elliptic springs at the front, and a stronger frame. A redesigned cylinder-head helped produce between 28 and 30 b.h.p. at 3600 r.p.m. Most had full pressure lubrication to cope with the extra power, which sufficed to give a guaranteed 75 m.p.h. The weight was only $11\frac{1}{2}$ cwt. This model was very popular in Britain, where it had almost no competition in its class, and what there was, was dearer. Vernon Balls, who at one time handled Amilcars, experimented with overhead valves and superchargers. Neither feature found its way into catalogued cars in Britain or France, though when made in Germany as the Pluto, and in Austria as the Grofri, superchargers could be had. These Amilcars were assembled in Italy as the Amilcar-Italiana. The final development of the type came in 1926 with the CGSs, the last 's' standing for *surbaissé*, these cars having a lowered chassis and radiator. Although they retained a two-bearing crankshaft, they were built for still more speed, with 'hotter' valve timing, up to 35 b.h.p. at 4500 r.p.m., 80 m.p.h., and a bigger

sump. Later cars had four forward speeds. A handful were made supercharged, when 40 b.h.p. was available, and pump cooling provided. A blown cabriolet won the 1927 Monte Carlo Rally. The CGS and the CGSs were in production until 1929, but were dropped then because such stark and sporting machinery had gone out of fashion in France.

5 TH. SCHNEIDER,
1928, France

This solid French fast tourer began life in 1922 as the 10CV, which was designed for side valves and offered only thus until 1924. In this form it was by no means a sporting car, but after its Besançon makers produced an alternative with overhead valves and 51 b.h.p. in 1924, as the 10/12 CV Sport, speed was added to its qualities of strength and endurance. This o.h.v. engine was designed by Côte. The combination resulted in a sixth place in the Le Mans 24-hour Race of 1926. With its vee radiator and Rudge-Whitworth wire wheels, it looked the part, though the old-fashioned cone clutch was retained until 1929, when a plate clutch was substituted. The Perrot brakes were given vacuum servo assistance in the same year. In other ways the model was conservative to the end, with its three-bearing crankshaft, separate gear-box carried in a sub-frame, and open propeller-shaft. A variety of axle ratios could be had, the 4·8 : 1 ratio enabling a speed of 76 m.p.h. to be attained at 3600 r.p.m. Cruising speed was 60 m.p.h. The sedan was good for 65 to 70 m.p.h. The controls were unusual, in that four little levers were provided, to regulate mixture, advance and retard of the spark, throttle, and oil feed to the rocker arms.

6 SARA, 1928, France

The SARA (Société des Applications du Refroidissement par Air) was the only air-cooled car to have even a modest success in France. Like Franklin in America, it achieved this by specializing, and evolving a practical product. It first saw the light in 1922 as an 1100 c.c. light four-cylinder machine. Its cooling system, which did not change, was very efficient, and consisted of a centrifugal turbine blower operating at $1\frac{1}{2}$ times engine speed, impelling air into a jacket around the separately cast, finned cylinders. Front suspension on the early cars was by transverse leaf springs. Thereafter, the SARA grew up. It acquired front-wheel brakes in 1924, and four forward speeds in 1927. New models appeared at the 1927 Paris Salon for 1928. These had six-cylinder engines, and half-elliptic instead of transverse front suspension. The six came in two forms; the P6 Touring and the SP7 Sport. The SARA, although reliable rather than fast, was entered energetically in competitions, and did fairly well. It competed at Le Mans regularly, beginning in 1923, and its best years were 1927 (when one of the new sixes in $1\frac{1}{2}$-litre form finished third in the Biennial Cup), and 1928, when a SARA was fourth in the Index of Performance. The make also took part in the 1929 Ulster Tourist Trophy Race. It was made in Britain as the Scotsman from Edinburgh, but the public did not want air cooling, and it died in the early 1930s.

7 LOMBARD AL3, 1928, France

Albert Lombard, a racing driver for Salmson, which had been easily the most successful manufacturer of cars in the 1100-c.c. voiturette racing class, gave his name in 1927 to a new line of cars that was designed by Vareilles. The machine that won the 1927 Coupé de la Commission Sportive at the Montlhéry Autodrome was called the AL2 'tank', after its streamlined body with faired-in wheels. It was extremely low built and compact, the engine being beside the driver. In AL3 form, with conventional, very pretty two-passenger sports bodywork, the Lombard went into limited production the same year. It was a most businesslike car in appearance, with dropped front axle, crab-tracked front wheels, and cycle-type wings. It weighed only 11 cwt.; so with a power output of 45 b.h.p. at 4800 r.p.m. unsupercharged, and 70 b.h.p. at 5500 r.p.m. blown, it was a formidable contender. The two overhead camshafts were shaft driven, but the cylinder head was fixed; a retrograde feature. Maximum speed was around 85 m.p.h. unsupercharged and 100 m.p.h. supercharged. The ensemble bore more than a passing resemblance to the more famous Salmson, not surprisingly. Some ninety-four were made of all types, including the experimental cars. The finest hour of the AL3 came in 1929, with victory in the Bol d'Or Race, in the hands of Dhome. In 1930 a straight-eight 3-litre machine for the 'touring' market was listed, Lombard in this following common practice at the time, but it did them no good. Production of the AL3 ceased, the BNC firm bought the last cars, raced them with BNC radiators, and sold them as the BNC AL3.

8 D'YRSAN, 1928, France

Raymond Siran was responsible for the sporting three-wheeled D'Yrsan of 1923; an altogether more sophisticated little beast than other French tricycles of the time, which were usually derived from the British Morgan (30). All D'Yrsans had water-cooled four-cylinder engines, supplied by Ruby in various sizes; they had three-speed gear-boxes made in unit with the engine, a plate clutch, shaft primary and chain final drive, and front-wheel brakes. They had, also, their own form of independent front suspension. The more powerful versions had overhead-valve engines that propelled them at up to 90 m.p.h. The first four-wheeled D'Yrsans appeared in 1927. The most common engine was a three-bearing 1100 c.c. unit which delivered up to 65 b.h.p. in supercharged form, but there was also an unblown engine with 35 b.h.p., and a smaller, 972 c.c. unit delivering 25 b.h.p. The independent front suspension became optional, normal half-elliptics being available. There was even a small sedan offered, and 1928 saw a six-cylinder engine, both signs of the times, but production of all types was strictly limited. All cars carried the 'Y' radiator motif of the make.

9 DELAGE DIS, 1928, France

From the time when his firm was founded in 1905, Louis Delage had a reputation for making fast cars, starting with stark and crude racing *voiturettes* and going on to such sophisticated complexities as the car that won the 1911 Coupe de *L'Auto* Race. Before 1914 his production cars tended to be pretty sober touring machines, but in 1924 he introduced a fast tourer in the finest French mould. Developed from the sluggish side-valve DE tourer of 1921, this new DI was merely the precursor of more exciting things. The DIS (or Sport) of 1924 had a high-lift camshaft, larger valves, a higher compression ratio, usually closer-ratio gears, a higher axle ratio, and sometimes a shorter chassis. The DISS of 1925 was given a lower chassis. The new DIS of 1927 was similar to the DISS, but invariably had a close-ratio gear-box. Maximum speed was over 70 m.p.h. The touring version of the DI series was called the Normale, or N. All were exceptionally well made, incorporating much aluminium in their construction. Earlier cars had open propeller-shafts, later enclosed in torque tubes. In spite of their excellence, the series was dropped in 1928 in favour of six-cylinder cars (already in the line) and eights of greater refinement and comfort (45).

10 BUGATTI TYPE 43, 1928, France

The pedigree of the Bugatti Type 43 was one of pure racing. It originated with the Type 35 Grand Prix car of 1924, built to the current 2-litre Grand Prix formula. The engine was basically that used in the 1922 and 1923 seasons. In 1924 the crankshaft was given ball and roller bearings. The car was, however, too slow to compete against the best of the 2-litre formula opposition, which had superchargers. This did not apply to its ultimate development, a *formule libre* machine with longer stroke, 2261 c.c. and Roots-type supercharger that came in 1926. This was the Type 35B model. At the end of 1926 the original 2-litre engine, now supercharged, was fitted to the Type 35C, another full racing car, which also had better cooling and brakes. The Type 43 Grand Sport of 1927 was the passenger car developed from the 35B. Naturally its performance was not quite on the latter's level; the 43 was longer and wider to accommodate a cramped four-passenger boat-tail body, the weight was 20 cwt. against 15 cwt., and power output was 115 b.h.p. against 140 b.h.p. At the same time, 70 m.p.h. was attainable in half a minute from a standstill, and the maximum speed was 112 m.p.h. Such a performance meant that this Bugatti was one of the fastest road cars of its day. The Type 43 was extremely safe at these speeds, but as W. F. Bradley said, it had 'all the characteristics of a racing car with a touring body', so it was mechanically very noisy. It was offered in 1930 in slightly less ferocious form, as the Type 43A with 'only' 100 b.h.p. and a rather more civilized roadster body, but the Bugatti sports-car fancier had to wait until 1932 for a machine with the normal refinements, the Type 55 (52).

11 RALLY TYPE ABC, 1928, France

The Rally was one of the better sporting *voiturettes* to emerge from the suburban workshops of Paris; in this case from Colombes, Seine. It started life as a cycle-car with an American vee-twin Harley-Davidson motor-cycle engine, but grew up to acquire a four-cylinder water-cooled engine in 1922. The Type ABC was a very pretty little car, new in 1927 and current until 1930. Its extremely low build was helped by a frame underslung below the axle at the rear. The front wheels were very crab-tracked, accentuating the car's business-like appearance. All had 1100 c.c. engines, first supplied by Chapuis-Dornier and then by SCAP. The latter, made in unit with the gear-box, came in three forms; the normal one with 30 b.h.p., the Grand Sport with 35 b.h.p. at 4200 r.p.m., providing (it is said) nearly 85 m.p.h., and the Cozette supercharged twin overhead-camshaft version, with 70 b.h.p. at 4650 r.p.m., that was claimed to propel the car at over 106 m.p.h. Even so, its main virtue was stamina. Milder Rallys were offered; there were three wheelbase lengths, sedans and cabriolets could be had, and there was even an ephemeral straight-eight, still of 1100 c.c.

12 MG 14/40, 1928. Great Britain

The origins of the MG go back to 1922, when Cecil Kimber, who ran the Morris Garages in Oxford, started fitting special bodies of a sporting aspect on to the standard Morris Oxford chassis. Other Morris dealers had done the same; Morris themselves had offered a fully-modified sports model until 1920. In 1924 the first MG to be offered under that name was produced by Kimber; in addition to notably handsome and dashing bodywork, it was slightly tuned (in respect of a polished and carefully assembled Oxford engine), had a higher axle ratio and flatter springs, and handled better than the Morris product. Christened the MG Super Sports, its rating was the same as that of the Oxford: 14/28 h.p. It catered perfectly for the growing market among ordinary men for cars of sporting appearance and mildly sporting behaviour, for in addition to looks and performance, it was easy to control, it was reliable, and it could use the nationwide Morris service network: qualities which true sports cars of the time could not match. When Morris went over from their famous 'bull-nose' to a flat radiator in 1927, Kimber followed suit. MGs were now heavier but their design was beginning to draw further away from its parentage. The 1928–9 cars were renamed the 14/40, though in fact power output was probably unchanged at around 35 b.h.p. Already in 1926, the MG had acquired vacuum servo brakes; not a feature of the contemporary Oxford. The 14/40 pulled a 4·42 : 1 axle ratio; its cylinder head was polished, as were the larger-than-standard ports; there were stronger valve springs, a different magneto and carburettor, and shock-absorbers front and rear. Two-passenger, four-passenger, and 'Salonette' bodies were listed, one of the latter being an odd affair with a boat-shaped tail. The two-passenger car weighed

19¾ cwt. complete. Maximum speed was around 65 m.p.h., and the acceleration was quite respectable for a basically touring design, 0–50 m.p.h. occupying twenty-five seconds. The braking betrayed the MG's ancestry more than other features of its performance, 90 ft. being needed in which to stop from 40 m.p.h. The last 14/40s were made in 1929, being superseded by the MG M-type Midget (39) and by the 18/80 MG (see 38), derivatives respectively of the Morris Minor and Morris Six.

13 AUSTIN SEVEN SUPER SPORTS and ULSTER, 1928–32, Great Britain

The Austin Seven light car, introduced in 1922, was a modern, efficient, simple, strong, cheap, thoroughly practical little vehicle, backed by good servicing facilities, that was intended to cater for the family man weary of the discomforts of the motor-cycle and sidecar or the cycle-car. Its engine, though only developing 10 b.h.p. at first, was capable of development; weight was only 9 cwt. at the same time; and there were front-wheel brakes (if not very good ones). There was sporting potential here; indeed, the Seven's first public appearance was at the 1922 Shelsley Walsh hill-climb. From 1923 the company took an interest in competitions; the Seven's first home win was in the Small Car Handicap at Brooklands track on Easter Monday, and its first foreign success was in that year's Italian Cycle-car Grand Prix at Monza. In order to take full advantage of the 750-c.c.

racing class, the engine of all cars was bored out by 2 mm., to make 747 c.c. The first sports Sevens to be offered to the public came in 1924; the manufacturers listed a short-lived two-passenger car with pointed tail and flared wings, its mildly-tuned engine providing 50 m.p.h. Gordon England Ltd. offered their very similar, but fabric-bodied, 'Cup' model, and also the very fierce Super Sports or Brooklands model, which was capable of 75 m.p.h. running stripped. In July 1928 Austin themselves introduced their second sports type, which they called the Super Sports. Works racing cars had been supercharged as early as 1925; the new production sports car was supercharged, too. It had a dropped front axle, a flatter front spring, and an engine with pressure-fed lubrication, a stronger, balanced crankshaft, special valve gear, camshaft and manifolds, a special cylinder head, and pump cooling. Power output was 27 b.h.p. at 4500 r.p.m. The maximum speed was around 70 m.p.h. By this time the standard touring car produced $12\frac{1}{2}$ b.h.p. The body of the new car was doorless, the sides being cut away. Early in 1930, a revised sports model was put into production. It could be had unsupercharged, in which case the engine developed 24 b.h.p. The chassis was lowered 3 in., and a close-ratio gear-box was supplied. Weight was $8\frac{1}{2}$ cwt. Maximum speed supercharged was now around 77 m.p.h., as power output had gone up to 33 b.h.p. at 5000 r.p.m. Works versions of the Super Sports won the 1929 and 1930 500-mile Race, and their class in the 1930 Brooklands Double 12-hour Race. In 1931 the production model was

renamed the Ulster, after the Austin's third and fourth places in the 1929 Ulster Tourist Trophy Race.

Few were made either of the Super Sports or of the Ulster: it was a specialized competition car of limited appeal, unlike the MG M-type Midget (39); though both were derived from popular economy cars.

14 OM TYPE 665 SUPERBA, 1928, Italy

The Officine Meccaniche of Brescia were an engineering firm, making ships, locomotives, and other heavy machinery, founded originally in Milan in 1899. They gained control of the Zust car in 1918, and in the same year designed a car of their own, a four-cylinder, 30-b.h.p. economy machine that was placed on the market three years later. Their most famous model was undoubtedly the 2-litre six cylinder that was derived from the Type 465 four (having two more cylinders of the same dimensions) and was introduced in 1923: the Type 665. Though of homely ancestry and designed primarily as a fast tourer, not a sports car, and in spite of a side-valve engine and the classic combination of a flexible chassis with stiff springing, the new car's performance and handling were first class (thanks in part to very good weight distribution) and were matched by the brakes, steering, and ease of control. Power output was 45 b.h.p. at 3500 r.p.m., and maximum speed was over 70 m.p.h. The type was first, second, and third in the Mille Miglia Race of 1927, and in the same year a faster version with two carburettors,

60 b.h.p. at 4000 r.p.m., and between 75 and 80 m.p.h. was introduced, based on the Mille Miglia cars. However, the OM was noted more for stamina than for speed, as shown by its performance at Le Mans in 1925 when it came fourth, and in 1926, when it was fifth and won the Rudge-Whitworth Cup, and in the Mille Miglia. In 1928 an OM finished second in the latter event and won its class. It won its class, too, in the 1928 Ulster Tourist Trophy Race, and the team prize in the 1929 Brooklands Double 12-hour Race. It was already being overshadowed by the 6C 1500 Alfa-Romeo, which in supercharged 1500 Super Sport form produced 75 b.h.p. The problem was to extract more power from somewhat rustic material. In Italy, a supercharger was fitted, and then the engine was increased in size to 2·2 litres (41), but the Alfas were by now going still faster, so it was to no avail. L. C. Rawlence, who had handled the OM since the four-cylinder was introduced in Britain, developed the Type 665 independently. R. F. Oats, working for Rawlence, experimented with an overhead-valve head in 1927, and Rawlence made six cars so fitted that produced 80 b.h.p. at 4500 r.p.m. A wider variety of body styles, too, was offered in Britain: open two- and four-passenger styles, a drop-head coupé, a sedan, and a sportsman's coupé.

15   ITALA TIPO 65S, 1928, Italy

Before the First World War, Itala had been one of the great names of Italy; one of the 'big three', with Fiat and Isotta-Fraschini, makers of glamorous racing cars, royal cars, and the machine that won the Peking–Paris Trial of 1907. Then the glory departed, and design stagnated in a rut. When Giulio Cesare Cappa, the talented creator of advanced Fiat and Aquila-Italiana racing cars, came to Itala and gave the firm its first modern design in the 1920s, it seemed that they might have a winner again. This Tipo 61 of 1924 was a 2-litre six cylinder, with pushrod-operated inclined overhead valves. The cylinder head was detachable, the block and pistons were of aluminium, the crankshaft had seven main bearings, the three-speed gear-box was replaced by one with four speeds in 1926, and there were servo-assisted brakes from the same year. Power output was 55 b.h.p. for the normal model, and 60 b.h.p. in sports form. The steering, plate clutch, and gear-box were easy and pleasant to use, and the handling was praised, but the car was too heavy, necessitating a low final drive ratio, and the maximum speed did not rise above 70 m.p.h. Nor was the power output as good as might be expected from the design and size of engine. Itala's answer was the Tipo 65S of 1928, first seen in the Le Mans 24-hour Race of that year, with Robert Benoist, 1927 World Champion, as one of the drivers. These cars (one of which is illustrated) were certainly not unduly heavy, with a chassis weight of little over 15 cwt., and their twin overhead-camshaft engines propelled even the production sports version at 84 m.p.h., but they could only manage eighth place. Significantly, they impressed with their quietness: this was still basically a touring design. The frame of the 65S was notably low-hung; the axles passed through holes in the side members. As in the case of the Tipo 61, touring and sports models were made, the former being called simply the Tipo 65. Both types were continued until about 1932. The last new Itala design was the Tipo 75 of that year, a 2·3-litre car of which the last were made in 1934.

16 FIAT TIPO 509S, 1928, Italy

The Fiat Tipo 509, which first saw the light at the Paris Salon of 1924, was a small car in the most modern idiom, with its tiny but high-revving and efficient engine, unit-construction gear-box with central gear-lever, low gearing in the interest of flexibility and hill-climbing, good four-wheel brakes, low-pressure tyres, soft suspension, and low price. It supplemented and later replaced the larger, less advanced Tipo 503, the previous Fiat 'small car'. No less than four body styles were offered. The publicity attending the launching of the 509 was impressive, including a tour of Italy by fifty examples. It was made available on hire-purchase by a finance company started by Fiat themselves, much as Ford had done earlier. Only a quarter of the price had to be put down, and no interest was payable. The result of all this was that by 1926, the 509 was the most common car on Italian roads. The 509A was an improvement, with better lubrication and different carburation. Chassis weight was a very reasonable $10\frac{1}{2}$ cwt.; a complete fabric-bodied sedan weighed only 17 cwt.

The chassis offered obvious sporting potential, and in 1926 there appeared the first sports derivative, the 509S. Current until 1928, its engine developed 27 b.h.p. at 4000 r.p.m. against the standard product's 22 b.h.p. at 3800 r.p.m., and provided 60 m.p.h. instead of 50. Though the car had a pretty body, some being like that of a minia-ture Alfa-Romeo (42), it retained the wide-ratio gear-box of its parent, and ran into bearing trouble. Still, sports Fiats competed in the first Mille Miglia of 1927, and more serious competition cars followed: the 509SM (Monza), with 30 b.h.p. and 65 m.p.h. and the supercharged 509MM (Mille Miglia), capable of nearly 80 m.p.h.

17 MERCEDES-BENZ SSK, 1929, Germany

The most famous car to come out of Germany in the 1920s—and most of this model *did* come out, since Germany was then a poor country whose citizens could not afford such luxuries—started life in 1925, as one of the last machines to bear the name Mercedes alone. This Type 630 was the creation of Ferdinand Porsche, who had come to Daimler as chief engineer in 1923. It was a luxury car, not a sports car, with a 6·4-litre engine rated at 24/100/140 P.S. in Germany and 33/140 h.p. in Britain, that propelled it at up to 85 m.p.h., which took a long time to attain even with the assistance of the supercharger. This was fitted simply to give an immensely heavy car a little more steam, not because Stuttgart saw it as anything approaching a sporting machine. The engine, with its overhead camshaft, and alloy cylinders with cast-iron liners, was modern enough, but the brakes and roadholding were terrible. By 1926 the merger between Daimler and Benz was resulting in a new line of cars called Mercedes-Benz, bearing the former's star inside the latter's laurel wreath, but the big Mercedes was not greatly changed. The Type K was lighter, shorter, and more powerful than the 630, with a 6240 c.c. engine rated at 24/110/160 P.S. (33/180 h.p.) and giving 98 m.p.h., but this merely made a dangerous car a death-trap: and it was, in fact, so nicknamed. However, a metamorphosis took place for 1927, with the Type S. This development of the Type K resulted in a sports car in the truest and finest sense; the first of what was in fact a new line. It was lighter and had a still bigger engine, enlarged to 6789 c.c. (26/120/180 P.S., 36/220 h.p.) giving 180 b.h.p. at 3000 r.p.m. running supercharged, and over 100 m.p.h. But this speed was attainable in comparative safety for the first time. A lower build and hydraulic shock-absorbers improved roadholding, the brakes were slightly better, while optional servo for the latter, a faster gear-change and lighter steering, with the inbred docility of its luxury antecedents, made the big car a bit less of a handful. In 1928 the Type S was developed into the Type SS (170/225 P.S., 38/250 h.p.). This car was subjected to further weight reduction, but still weighed 47 cwt. Its boosted, 225 b.h.p. engine, unchanged in cylinder dimensions, gave it a maximum speed of around 116 m.p.h. on the 2·75 : 1 final drive ratio. It had the reputation of not handling quite as well as the S. The most ferocious of the production models of the series followed in the same year, the SSK (which is illustrated). The K stood for Kurz, or short, and in the abbreviated chassis was 250 b.h.p., providing 126 m.p.h. The SSKL (Kurz, Leicht—Short, light) of 1931, with 300 b.h.p., was a machine of which only a handful were built. Fewer than 300 cars of the S series were made —146 of the S, 112 of the SS, and 33 of the SSK. Yet, they made a far deeper mark on competitions than their numbers suggested. They were raced successfully in Europe until 1934 and in South America until 1938, even in events of Grand Prix status. Their most famous victories were in the German Grands Prix of 1927 and 1928, the Ulster Tourist Trophy Race of 1929, and the Mille Miglia of 1931.

18, 19 AUSTRO-DAIMLER ADR SPORT and ADR6 BERGMEISTER, 1929, 1933, Austria

The ancestry of the last, and some say the finest, model to come from the Wiener-Neustadt works of Austria's foremost motor manufacturer dated back to 1923. Ferdinand Porsche's Type ADM was a fine fast tourer with a single overhead-camshaft six-cylinder, 2½-litre engine utilizing aluminium cylinders and cast-iron detachable liners, in line with modern aviation practice. In its ultimate guise this model became the ADMIII, which in short-chassis sports form (2) was a 100 m.p.h. car with 100 b.h.p. 3-litre engine and fine steering and brakes. The ADMIII won the team prize in the 1928 Ulster Tourist Trophy Race. Only the chassis, still with cantilever rear springs, was left behind in this development. However, with the arrival of Karl Rabe, a tubular backbone frame with independent rear suspension, similar enough to the well-known Tatra design for the latter firm to sue for infringement, was introduced. The brakes had servo assistance. In his ADR series, Rabe installed the Porsche engine into his very advanced frame, making a superb combination. But there was to be a further transition. In 1931 a new engine was applied to the Rabe chassis, and the outcome was the magnificent Bergmeister ADR6. This 3·6-litre unit, basically similar to the original Porsche design, developed 120 b.h.p. at 3600 r.p.m. giving the new car a maximum speed of 94 m.p.h. with its normal heavy German cabriolet or convertible bodies. Factory tuning made the Bergmeister go still faster, in spite of a crankshaft with only three main bearings. Two chassis lengths were available. Fifty Bergmeisters were built, from 1931 to 1937, delivery continuing for two years after manufacture had stopped at Wiener-Neustadt and the Steyr-Daimler-Puch combine had been formed. Rabe himself later went to work for Porsche. Probably the most famous car to make use of Bergmeister components was Hans von Stuck's special racing machine in which he won the 1930 European hill-climbing championship. It had an engine of ADMIII dimensions tuned to give 120 b.h.p. at 5500 r.p.m., and very big brakes, but this engine was replaced by a Bergmeister unit developed to provide 200 b.h.p.

20 DUPONT MODEL G LE MANS SPEEDSTER, 1929, U.S.A.

DuPont Motors Inc. were unusual among American manufacturers in that their emphasis was always on speedsters, from their first year of 1920. They even went as far as to make three toy speedsters in 1928, with Henderson four-cylinder motor-cycle engines and three forward speeds, 6 ft. long and allegedly capable of up to 70 m.p.h. However, their most famous car of this type was undoubtedly the Model G Speedster of 1929, although it was only one of twelve models that year. The name DuPont had been chosen deliberately, as being excitingly 'foreign' and therefore luxurious, and the new car backed up this effect strikingly in its appearance. The two-passenger body, designed by the Merrimac Body Company, was of French Amilcar inspiration, with its straight, narrow wings and small frontal area, to which the profiled Woodlite headlamps and radiator grille (one of the world's first) contributed. The eight-cylinder Continental engine developed 140 b.h.p. at 3600 r.p.m., providing just under 100 m.p.h. The four-speed gear-box was unusual in American cars of the time, but top was a 3·75 : 1 overdrive ratio. Normal motoring was done on the 5·3 : 1 third, on which 5–70 m.p.h. was available. The company entered two special cars in the 1929 Le Mans 24-hour Race. Their aluminium pointed-tail speedster bodies accommodated four passengers, to fit the race regulation. Only one DuPont started; the car driven by the amateur Charles Moran. It was running in eighth place and was leading all the other American contestants with an average speed of 72 m.p.h. when its ballast, breaking through the floor, put pressure on and broke the transmission. This performance was all the more remarkable when it is remembered that even the standard two-passenger Model G weighed almost 2 tons. The Le Mans cars had a shorter chassis and a higher compression ratio than the ordinary car, with a clear maximum speed of 100 m.p.h. The Le Mans competition type was a listed model for 1930, but production ceased altogether in 1932.

21 **CORD L29,** 1929, U.S.A.

Errett Lobban Cord, President of the Auburn Automobile Company (66) and of Duesenberg Inc. (78), by 1929 had a distinctive car in the medium-price range and one at the summit of the luxury range. He wanted a truly unusual machine somewhere in between, and the designer Cornelius van Ranst, who had worked with Harry Miller, America's highly successful exponent since 1924 of front-wheel drive racing cars, gave it to him. Miller became associated with Cord. Using Miller patents, Van Ranst produced the Cord L29; America's first production front-wheel drive car. With the DuPont Model G (20), the Cord was also the first car to have a radiator grille. The Lycoming side-valve straight-eight engine was the same as that fitted to the Auburn 8/115 and 8/120 (66), reversed in the chassis. A high-compression cylinder-head was offered as an option. The engine, transmission, differential,

and front brake assembly were in unit with the drive-shafts, mounted in the frame. There was a tubular front axle with the Lockheed internal expanding hydraulic brakes mounted inboard. Four body styles were available on a very stiff chassis. The Cord was a big car, but its low build and appearance, facilitated by front-wheel drive, long hood and long wings, made for an elegant line. At the same time, ground clearance was good. In 1932 came a new engine with a bigger bore, and 125 b.h.p. at 3600 r.p.m., but the L29 was *too* different, in specifications and handling qualities, to be commercially acceptable. It went out of production that year.

22 **TRACTA,** 1929–30, France

During 1927 the engineer J. A. Gregoire of Asnières raced a front-wheel drive design which he displayed at the Paris Salon late that year. Its first appearance had been at the Le Mans 24-hour Race in the summer. Gregoire was one of the first motor manufacturers in the world to put a front-wheel drive car into production. The constant-velocity universal joint design was by P. Fenaille, and was at first driven by a four-cylinder SCAP-made proprietary engine of 1100 c.c., reversed in the chassis. A Cozette supercharger was optional. Ignition was by magneto. Power output of the 1927 Le Mans car was 37 b.h.p. at 4300 r.p.m., with a maximum speed of over 85 m.p.h. The gear-box was mounted in front of the engine. There was independent front suspension by a transverse leaf spring, and inboard, hydraulically-operated front-wheel brakes. The gear-change was by a dashboard-mounted lever. By 1929 the SCAP-engined 1600 c.c. version, that had replaced the original 1100 c.c. model, was good for nearly 70 m.p.h., but a low-hung, crab-tracked 1928 sports model with engine dimensions bringing it within the 1½-litre class would reach 80 m.p.h. In 1929 Gregoire made a two-stroke design with supercharged, four-cylinder eight-piston engine by Cozette. Tractas competed at Le Mans for no less than eight years running, from 1927 to 1934, winning their class in 1929 and 1930, but attractive coupé as well as two-passenger bodies were offered, and in 1930 a real concession was made to the sybarites in the form of the 15CV model. This had a flexible, silent side-valve six-cylinder American engine made by Continental, of 2·7 litres' cubic capacity, and three forward speeds. Two chassis lengths were available. The last engine used by Tracta was the 3-litre, six-cylinder Hotchkiss unit (80). The idiosyncratic Tracta was made until 1936; a surprisingly long lease of life for so unconventional a car. Still, between 1927 and 1932, its hey-day, fewer than 100 were built.

23   ARIÈS 3-LITRE SPORT, 1929, France

Ariès, motor manufacturers since 1903, had begun to concentrate upon com-mercial vehicles just before the First World War, and continued to devote most of their efforts to this line after peace returned. However, during the war they made Hispano-Suiza aero engines under licence, and their new 3-litre Sport, current from 1925 to 1930 and first seen in the Grand Prix de Tourisme in 1924, reflected the Hispano design in its shaft-driven overhead-camshaft engine. Its stroke was the same as that of the contemporary tour-ing side-valve Ariès 15CV, but the bore was reduced from 85 mm. to fit the 3-litre racing class. The Sport also had the four-wheel brakes at first lacking in the touring machine. Power output with a 7 : 1 compression ratio was up-wards of 92 b.h.p. in 1926. There were four forward speeds in a separate gear-box. The 1926 Le Mans 24-hour Race car had a lowered chassis. The 1927 Le Mans race saw the Ariès giving the winning 3-litre Bentley a run for its money. The Sport's last competition appearance—by now with a bore of 85 mm. and 3·2 litres—was in the Grand Prix of Europe in 1930, when it finished. Another successful Ariès was the overhead-camshaft 1100 c.c. model that, in racing form, won its class at San Sebastian in 1924 and in the 24-hour Race at Spa in 1926, 1927, and 1928. It also took home the Florio Cup in 1927. The last new Ariès design before pro-duction ceased in 1932 was the four-cylinder touring car, with overhead inlet and side exhaust valves, designed by Toutée, formerly of Chenard-Walcker.

24   BENTLEY 4½-LITRE, 1929, Great Britain

The 4½-litre Bentley had been intro-duced in 1927 because the basically similar 3-litre, which had been upholding the Bentley name since 1921, was being outclassed in terms of performance by cars such as the French Lorraine-Dietrich in racing and by the 30/98 h.p. Vauxhall on the road. The first few cars consisted simply of a 3-litre chassis with the new, larger engine installed, giving 110 b.h.p. at 3500 r.p.m. and 92 m.p.h. Most cars had their own transmission and longer, stronger chassis. The $4\frac{1}{2}$-litre (see illustration) had a highly successful competition career, but after the Le Mans 24-hour Race of 1928, which it won only narrowly, it was clear that more speed was necessary. The Bentley company's answer was the Speed Six (25), but H. R. S. Birkin, one of the amateurs who raced Bentleys, believed that the existing $4\frac{1}{2}$-litre could be made to do what was required by means of supercharging. While Bentley helped Birkin, the former put his money (rightly, as it turned out) on the Speed Six, and ran no 'works' supercharged racing cars himself. The first supercharged car appeared early in 1929, but it was dogged by teething troubles, mainly concerned with lubrication, arising from the supercharging of an engine not designed for it. By late 1930 —after Bentley had withdrawn from racing—the lubrication problems had been solved by the use of a larger sump ribbed for cooling. The four racing cars run by Birkin and Miss Dorothy Paget were capable of speeds up to 125 m.p.h. But they had little luck: their finest hour was undoubtedly Birkin's second place in the 1930 French Grand Prix, against full Grand Prix cars. The car was put into limited production in 'cooler' form by Bentley. Fifty machines were made. The Roots-supercharged engine had a stronger crankshaft, which was also

fitted to subsequent unsupercharged $4\frac{1}{2}$-litre engines. Power output was 175 b.h.p., and the maximum speed 103 m.p.h. They were remarkably smooth and flexible, with 10 m.p.h. possible in top gear.

25 BENTLEY SPEED SIX,
1929–30, Great Britain

The original, 3-litre, four-cylinder Bentley first sold in 1921 was undoubtedly a sporting machine in character and intention, but it was versatile, in that the engine was notably flexible. A long chassis and lower gear ratios were offered to customers who wanted to fit less sporting bodies. These clients came to outnumber the sportsmen, and the formal or otherwise heavy bodies some fitted to their cars killed the latters' characteristic performance. Walter Owen Bentley therefore introduced, late in 1925, his Big Six or Standard Six. Power output was 140 b.h.p. enabling it to reach 85 m.p.h. It retained the basic engine design, with four valves and two plugs per cylinder. Production ceased in 1930. Meanwhile, however, the four-cylinder development of the 3-litre, the $4\frac{1}{2}$-litre, was finding increasingly formidable opposition in competitions—it had only just won the Le Mans 24-hour Race in 1928. Something faster was needed, and Bentley at the end of the year introduced the Speed Model on the six-cylinder chassis, usually known as the Speed Six. From an engine of the same dimensions between 160 and 180 b.h.p. was extracted at a characteristically modest 3500 r.p.m. The Speed Six shared the vacuum servo-assisted brakes and the dual magneto and coil ignition of the current Standard Six. Maximum speed in open four-passenger form, when the car weighed between 2 and $2\frac{1}{4}$ tons, was 92 m.p.h. A Speed Six won the Le Mans 24-hour Race in 1929, in the hands of Woolf Barnato and H. R. S. Birkin, and the same machine carried off Le Mans in the following year, driven by Barnato and Glen Kidston. Another Speed Six was second in the latter year, and won the Brooklands Double 12-hour Race in 1930. The winner at Le Mans in 1929 and 1930 went on to win the Brooklands 500-mile Race of 1931, as a stripped single seater. The Le Mans team Speed Sixes had 200 b.h.p. on tap, and upwards of 125 m.p.h., dependent on the axle ratio and amount of road equipment carried. The model had done all that was asked of it in an exemplary fashion; a highly successful design of which 170-odd were made up to 1930.

26 H.E. SIX, 1929, Great Britain

Herbert Engineering Ltd., who took their initials for the name of their car, were small-scale assemblers of high-quality, expensive, completely straightforward fast touring machines, most noted for their rakishly handsome good looks. The four-cylinder, side-valve model of around 2 litres' cubic capacity, with separate gear-box, was their classic model. Late in 1927, for 1928, they introduced a new six-cylinder car alongside the four, in deference to fashion, but it retained its companion's qualities. The 2·3-litre engine, which

used a Whatmough-designed alloy cylinder-head and inclined valves, at first developed 55 b.h.p. at 3800 r.p.m.; an output later boosted to 60 b.h.p. Bodies were generally fabric-covered. on Weymann principles. A short-chassis sports version of the Six appeared in 1929, and was good for 80 m.p.h. The touring car would reach 70 m.p.h. In all, only sixty-four Sixes were built, and each was sold with a five years' guarantee.

27 RILEY BROOKLANDS, 1929, Great Britain

Percy Riley believed that the average small family car of the middle 1920s was unnecessarily heavy, wasteful of space, and mechanically inefficient. His answer was the Riley Nine, of which prototypes were running in 1926 and production models on sale late in 1927. In its combination of advanced design, lightness, refinement, and low price, there was nothing like it on the road, The engine employed two high camshafts to drive the overhead valves by rockers and short pushrods. This arrangement allowed well-shaped combustion chambers and high revolutions, which in turn produced the fairly high power output for an 1100 c.c. engine of 29 b.h.p. at 4500 r.p.m. At the same time, reliability and flexibility were not lost. The crankshaft was a balanced and very stiff component, so having only two main bearings was of no importance under normal stresses. The normal Monaco fabric sedan body, mounted on a rigid frame, was a strong construction, in which all passengers sat within the wheelbase, with their feet in wells in the floor. Light weight and a low centre of gravity made for good roadholding, as did the excellent steering and suspension. The total weight of the Monaco four-passenger sedan was only $17\frac{1}{2}$ cwt. and maximum speed was a lively 60 m.p.h., which was better than any other production 1100 c.c. sedan could manage. This remarkable little car, the first truly modern light-car design, was an obvious basis for a sports car, which was being developed by J. G. Parry-Thomas as early as 1927. After Thomas' death, Reid Railton of Thomson & Taylor, the engineering firm at Brooklands track, took over. The Brooklands model Riley Nine, or Speed Model, was first made by Thomson & Taylor, then by Riley Ltd. It went into production in 1929; a sports racing car with few concessions to less specialized uses. The two-bearing crankshaft was ultimately to prove the limiting factor, but the engine was notably responsive to tuning. The standard model Brooklands engine gave 50 b.h.p. at 5000 r.p.m. There were four separate exhaust pipes in the interests of good extraction. A special close-ratio gear-box with remote control was fitted, and a final drive ratio of 4·77 : 1 instead of the touring chassis'. 5·2 : 1. The frame was shortened to 8 ft., and lowered even more. Maximum speed was 80 m.p.h., with 70 m.p.h. available in third gear. Pure racing versions went considerably faster. The suspension was harsh and the body sketchy, so this was no car for touring. It gained class wins in the Ulster T.T. Race and Irish Grand Prix of 1930, and an outright win in the 1932 Ulster T.T.

28 LEA-FRANCIS HYPER SPORTS, 1929, Great Britain

This fine specialized sports racing car was the ultimate development of a long line of spartan little machines from Coventry, unusually sporting performers all, that had begun with the 10 h.p. Lea-Francis light car of 1923. Two years later came the ephemeral L-type sports model with $1\frac{1}{2}$-litre Meadows 4ED engine, rated at 12/40 h.p. In 1928 there arrived the 12/40 h.p. P-type. This broke from the Lea-Francis tradition of stark, uncomfortable sporting cars, with its wider chassis and roomy four-passenger bodies. It was a full-scale touring car with a 60 m.p.h. maximum, which most 1928 cars of 2 litres' cubic capacity were hard put to it to attain. In 1928 the 12/40 was supplemented by the 12/50, with a more potent version of the 4ED unit, but in the same year a new range was introduced alongside them. The most distinguished of this Hyper series was the S-type sports racing car (see illustration). Its Meadows engine, Cozette supercharged, developed 61 b.h.p. at 4100 r.p.m. in production form. Maximum speed was 95 m.p.h., with the standard two-passenger, fabric-covered body. The hood was of metal. The axle ratio was to choice, between 4·7 and 3·9 : 1. Alongside the S-type were two other Hypers, a four-passenger fabric sedan and open tourer, capable of 85 and 90 m.p.h. respectively. The three Hypers all had inclined radiators, but some non-supercharged cars, not Hypers, also had this feature. The S-type won the 1928 Ulster Tourist Trophy Race, its class in the Le Mans 24-hour Race of

1928 and 1929, and the 1928 200-mile Race of the Junior Car Club at Brooklands. The works team cars were developed for these competitions, with a specially massive crankshaft, roller-bearing big ends, tubular steel connecting rods, special valves and timing, a more powerful supercharger and stronger axles. They weighed $19\frac{3}{4}$ cwt., and their engines developed 79 b.h.p. at 4500 r.p.m., which gave them a maximum speed of around 100 m.p.h. The Hyper was made until 1932. During this, 189 S-types were sold.

29 ALVIS FRONT-WHEEL DRIVE, 1929, Great Britain

This model of Alvis, one of the world's first production cars to have front-wheel drive, had its origins in the special competition machines built by the company in 1925 to offer effective opposition in the 1500 c.c. *voiturette* class to the formidable Darracq and A.C. racers. Front-wheel drive was adopted in order to save weight, and improve roadholding. This car had a duralumin frame, a supercharged pushrod overhead-valve engine, and semi-independent front suspension on an adaptation of the De Dion principle. Rear suspension was non-independent. The type was listed for sale in 1926 as the 12/80 h.p., with a 100 m.p.h. guarantee, but none was sold. Cars built in 1926 to the new $1\frac{1}{2}$-litre Grand Prix formula had straight-eight horizontal-valve engines, but the same suspension layout, while the 1927 Grand Prix machines with eight-cylinder twin overhead-camshaft en-

gines had fully independent front suspension on the lines of the production cars to follow, and unchanged rear suspension. These cars afforded the company plenty of experience for their catalogued front-wheel drive model, which appeared in 1928. They differed again in detail, with four-cylinder engines using some parts from the firm's standby, the 12/50 h.p., but with a single overhead camshaft instead of pushrod overhead valves, and an engine reversed in the chassis. The Roots-type supercharger was optional. The standard body styles were a two-passenger, an open four-passenger, and a four-passenger sedan, all with fabric bodies, on two chassis lengths. The open four-passenger car weighed 25 cwt. Fifty b.h.p. was available unsupercharged, and 75 b.h.p. blown. In either case, 85 m.p.h. was obtainable, but stripped for racing and with the optional 4·55 : 1 axle ratio, the two-passenger model's maximum was 100 m.p.h. The brakes were first class, while the combination of low centre of gravity, independent suspension, and front-wheel drive provided very good roadholding. This model, built in 1928-9, won its class in the Le Mans 24-hour Race of 1928, and came second in that year's Ulster Tourist Trophy Race. However, an altogether more potent machine appeared in 1929; with a straight-eight engine of 1491 c.c. with the same cylinder dimension as the Grand Prix cars of 1926-7. It was put into limited production until 1930 as the Ulster model, which was only offered supercharged, and carried a 100 m.p.h. guarantee. Power output was 125 b.h.p., and maximum speed 110 m.p.h. These cars proved themselves the equals of the

Alfa-Romeo from Italy (26) in speed, stamina, and handling, but Alvis did not persist with them. The front-wheel drive cars were expensive, complex, unconventional, and called for skill in their drivers. They were difficult to maintain and temperamental. For these reasons the Alvis gamble of offering a model intended solely for sportsmen failed, and threatened to upset the company's image. The faithful old 12/50 had been dropped for 1930, leaving only the comparatively luxurious six-cylinder Silver Eagle in the Alvis range of touring cars, but it was hurriedly reinstated for 1931, after the front-wheel drive design was abandoned.

30, 31 **MORGAN AERO** and **SUPER SPORTS,** 1929, 1934, Great Britain

The Morgan was Britain's most popular three-wheeled car, at a time when taxation favoured three against four wheels, and there was therefore plenty of competition. A combination of simplicity (and consequently reliability and ease of maintenance) with an excellent power-to-weight ratio, fierce acceleration at low engine speeds, better-than-average handling, economy of running, and low price provided an unbeatable recipe for cheap speed, at the expense of exposure, noise, and a harsh ride (which the dedicated enthusiast who bought Morgans accepted). The little beast was born in 1910 as a much tamer, even simpler single-passenger cycle-car (the minimal motor-car of the time) with a single- or twin-cylinder motor-cycle-type air-cooled engine of 1100 c.c. by J.A.P.

There was tiller steering. However, even this early primitive had the Morgan's classic features of independent front suspension by sliding pillars inside coil springs, two forward speeds by dog clutches and separate chains, and a tubular backbone frame. Seating for two passengers and (direct) wheel steering had arrived by 1911, still with a weight of only 3 cwt., and the fundamental specification was complete. Maximum speed was 55 m.p.h., which was good for a normal car of 4 litres' cubic capacity, and acceleration vastly superior. The basic design was sporting enough, but from 1914 special sports variants were introduced, starting with the Grand Prix model. The Aero was a development of the Grand Prix, introduced in 1919. The Family and De Luxe models were offered beside it. In 1920 four forward speeds were to be had as an extra, but were not common. Electric lighting was optional a year later, and standard in 1925. Front-wheel brakes could be specified in 1923, as could a dynamo and balloon tyres a year later. Even electric starting, a true concession to the sybarites, was available in 1925, and in the following year all types except the very cheapest had front-wheel brakes. Steering reduction, and three forward speeds with reverse, were offered for the first time in 1927. A wide choice of engines with air or water cooling was to be had in these years. A new water-cooled overhead-valve 1096 c.c. J.A.P. unit or a Blackburne were provided with Aeros in 1925. The latter gave 45 b.h.p. and 72 m.p.h. By 1927 the choice lay between the J.A.P. overhead-valve or side-valve engine, or the water-cooled Anzani Vulpine. The standard axle ratios were

4·5 or 5 : 1. The new Aero Super Sports of 1928 with 10/40 h.p. J.A.P. afforded an 80 m.p.h. maximum with a weight of 8 cwt., and shock-absorbers on all wheels. Thereafter, however, Morgans were forced increasingly to compromise with the new breed of far more civilized, if less exciting, cheap sports cars typified by the M.G. M-type Midget (39) that were luring their market away. A three-speed sliding-pinion gear-box of conventional design was found on all models from 1931, a four-cylinder Ford engine was introduced for 1934, and the last twins were made in as late as 1946. The last truly sporting Morgan three-wheeler was the Super Sports with a 40 b.h.p. Matchless vee-twin engine, air or water cooled, with overhead-valve or side-valve motor respectively. This unit drove through a friction clutch to a three-speed-and-reverse gear-box, and thence by a single chain to the rear wheel. A self-starter was provided. This car came to an end with the withdrawal of the Matchless engine.

32 STANDARD AVON SPECIAL, 1929, Great Britain

At the 1927 Olympia Motor Show in London, the Standard Motor Company, who had made a variety of medium-sized, middle-class cars since the end of the First World War, reverted to a pre-1914 Standard type; a really small, cheap vehicle, but now to be manufactured in mass quantities as serious competition in the market dominated by the Austin Seven and the Morris Minor. The 8·9 h.p., 1159 c.c.

Fulham utility sedan, the Falmouth de luxe sedan, and the Coleshill and Selby open cars made up the range, to be replaced in 1928 by a line on a longer wheelbase, making them less stubby-looking, and with a larger, bored-out engine, the 9·9 h.p. At the same time, the firm offered their first catalogued sports model, with body built by the specialist coachbuilder Gordon England, on the earlier, smaller-engined chassis. It was a normal chassis mildly tuned, joining the swelling ranks of cheap cars for the ordinary man who wanted to look excitingly sporting without actually *being* sporting. It could also be had with a supercharger. Meanwhile, the New Avon Body Company of Warwick had been making bodies to replace Standard's normal styles; rather pedestrian, four-square shapes. In 1929 they were joined by Alan Jensen (88), who was responsible for the first of the Standard Avon Specials. These had a long, low, elegant look quite foreign to Standard's family cars or even to the Gordon England Sports model. Avon, and before them the Swallow Coachbuilding Company (98) made a great success out of exploiting—by offering a cheap alternative to them—the sawn-off, boxy, ugly bodies worn by the typical small family car of the time. In the case of the Standard Avon Special, the new 'look' was aided by use of the still longer Big Nine chassis of 1930. This had a bevel axle instead of an underslung worm final drive. The standard Coventry product was further lowered in appearance by underslung springs, a long hood, and a heavily-valanced body. Open two-passenger and fixed-head coupé sports types were offered. The upper car shown is the prototype. The 16 h.p. 2-litre six-cylinder chassis was also given the Avon 'treatment', and was capable of around 75 m.p.h. Mechanically, the smaller car was altered in respect of a raised compression ratio, a larger choke tube in the carburettor, and a top-gear ratio of 4·6 : 1 instead of 5 : 1. However, the other ratios were not changed, and this gear-box remained very 'gappy'. The Big Nine had a wider track than its predecessor, and was given coil ignition. The Avons followed suit. A four-speed gear-box was eventually provided. In 1932 Jensen left Avon, and the old line of Specials died. A range of much more sybaritic, opulent bodies, styled by Charles Beauvais, was substituted, leaving no trace of the Jensen cars.

33, 34 ROLLS-ROYCE PHANTOM I and PHANTOM II CONTINENTAL, 1929, 1933, Great Britain

These machines, the last Rolls-Royces built primarily for high performance, had their origins in the New Phantom of 1925, a modernized Silver Ghost, replacing the car that had made the reputation of the company over nearly twenty years. It had a more powerful, overhead-valve engine developing 100 b.h.p., and a plate clutch, though it was heavier in weight, handling, and appearance. Maximum speed was 75–80 m.p.h. A few examples of a Continental variant were built on a shorter chassis and carrying a brief two-passenger body with flared wings. This car could reach 90 m.p.h. The Phantom II replaced the Phantom I in 1929. This car was extensively redesigned, incorporating unit construction of engine and gear-box, an open propeller-shaft instead of torque tube, half-elliptic springs instead of cantilevers at the rear, and centralized chassis lubrication. This was an 85 m.p.h. car with a pleasant clutch and gear-box, and better steering and roadholding than the original Phantom. Two chassis lengths were offered: 12 ft. 6 in., or 12 ft. In 1933 came synchromesh between top and third gear, extended to second gear in 1935, the last year of production of the Phantom II. Meanwhile, a new Continental model had been introduced on the Phantom II chassis. Like its predecessor, it was intended specifically for high-speed foreign touring. The short 12-ft. wheelbase was used. The compression ratio was raised to give 130 b.h.p. at 3000 r.p.m., the steering column was raked and the springs flattened for a lowering effect, double shock-absorbers were fitted to the front axle, and a higher axle ratio was employed. Two-and-a-half tons of motor-car could be accelerated from rest to 60 m.p.h. in under twenty seconds, and the maximum speed was 92 m.p.h., with 68 m.p.h. available in third gear.

35 FIAT TIPO 525S, 525SS, 1929, 1930, Italy

In 1927, Fiat, Italy's biggest motor manufacturers, decided (like other firms at the same time) to fight the American competitors who were taking so much of the home and export market by offering the same kind of big, cheap, flexible six-cylinder car—while continuing their own small cars. Overhead valves were dropped in favour of side valves in the new, slow-turning engines, but four forward speeds in the European tradition were retained, as were Fiat's light steering, good handling, and good brakes. The biggest of the range was the Tipo 525 of 1929, which differed from the rest in being intended as an exceptionally silent and comfortable machine in the luxury category in character if not in price, for a comparatively restricted market. The normal model had an engine developing 70 b.h.p. at 3400 r.p.m., pulling a 4·7 : 1 axle ratio. The mechanical brakes were given vacuum servo assistance, then (in 1931, the last year of production) hydraulic brakes were substituted. The latter had been tested in a specially lowered and 'hotted-up' car entered in the 1929 International Alpine Trial. From this machine there emerged a small series of Tipo Spinto (tuned) cars, or 525SS, one of which is illustrated (bottom). Apart from a lowered chassis with a 3·8 : 1 axle ratio, that wore a short open four-passenger sports body in the English tradition and wire wheels, the engine was modified in respect of a raised compression ratio, twin-choke carburettor, and revised inlet manifold. The 525S (top) had a slightly shorter chassis than the standard 525.

36 MINERVA AKS, 1929, Belgium

Sylvain de Jong made bicycles from 1897, then became interested in power attachments, first offering French De Dion Bouton engines and then his own. He progressed to motor-cycles, making a most advanced unit with mechanically-operated overhead inlet valves in 1903, but built his first experimental car in 1900. By 1901 passenger cars were in production. Late in 1908, De Jong adopted the American Charles Yale Knight's double sleeve-valve engine, and from 1910 to the end all his cars had it. The design was particularly suited to the luxury chassis which were henceforth Minerva's bread and butter, because of its silence of operation, smoothness and flexibility, but it could also, as proved by De Jong in Belgium and Panhard, Peugeot, and Voisin in France, be made to provide sustained high-speed reliability. The mainstay of the Minerva line, and its biggest representative, was the 30CV of 1919, current until 1927. The six-cylinder engine had dimensions of 90 × 140 mm., giving 5·3 litres. This car was replaced in 1927 by the 32CV, or AK model, with 95 mm. bore, 4·9 litres, very good vacuum servo-assisted brakes, and a maximum speed of 70 m.p.h. in 47-cwt. limousine form. In turn, the 32CV was superseded in 1929 by the 40CV AL, a 6·6-litre straight-eight. Meanwhile, however, the 32CV AK appeared in AKS or Speed Model form. This was a formidable machine with high-compression engine, lightweight sleeves, connecting rods and pistons, a power output of 150 b.h.p., and a maximum speed of 90 m.p.h. To complete an increasingly complex picture, one other car should be noted: in 1930, a small 4-litre eight, the 75 × 112 mm. 28CV, for clients whose fortunes were being eroded by the Great Depression. This car produced 90 b.h.p. at 3200 r.p.m. and 80 m.p.h. in normal form, while the shorter, sports version of 1933 gave 105 b.h.p.

Minerva's publicity concentrated on demonstrating long-distance speed and dependability. In Andre Pisart's hands, a 28CV in 1930 covered the distance from Ostend to Marseilles and back in just over $32\frac{1}{2}$ hours. In the following year an AK, setting out to achieve over 10,000 miles in under ten days, in fact motored 6400 miles in 142 hours—a little over six days. This time represented an average speed overall of 48 m.p.h., much of the distance being over bad roads. The great series of Minervas that began in 1919 with the 30CV ended in 1934 when the firm joined forces with Imperia. In the interim, they had built up an immense store of goodwill among the wealthy everywhere, particularly in America and in the royal families of Belgium, Holland, Luxembourg, Scandinavia, and the Eastern countries.

37 JORDAN SPEEDWAY EIGHT, 1930, U.S.A.

Edward S. Jordan started to make the cars bearing his name in 1916. They were assembled machines of exceptionally good quality, reliable and quiet, not specially fast, usually with aluminium bodies. Jordan's genius showed itself in his 1919 range. It was a genius for salesmanship, not technical expertise. He aimed his advertising at women, whom he saw as the prime influence in car purchase. His promotion therefore broke right away from technicalities. Jordan body styles had light, attractive lines, and brilliant names backed by equally brilliant advertising copy that was intended to invoke a spirit of adventure. The Playboy roadster, a type retained for several years, named after J. M. Synge's *The Playboy of the*

Western World, was the most famous. Later came the Blueboy and the Tomboy. The first eight-cylinder model was the 1925 Great Line Eight. There was something more masculine in these names, and from around 1927 the Jordan image began to come down to earth in other ways. The little Custom Six of that year, with its wheelbase of under 9 ft. and underslung worm drive, was a serious attempt to introduce a small car on European lines to the American market. It lasted only two seasons, to be replaced by the longer Cross Country Six. After Jordan had retired from the company, it brought out a machine that sought to emulate the contemporary high-performance luxury car from Europe. This was the Speedway Eight, a very big car on a wheelbase of over 12 ft. with a Continental engine developing 114 b.h.p. The aero associations of the earlier Air Line Eight were revived in this car, with its clean modern lines (accentuated by dropshaped Woodlite headlamps, aerofoil running-boards, concealed radiator cap, and twin trumpet horns), and its full range of aircraft instruments, including altimeter, compass, revolution counter, and aero-type spark, throttle, and choke controls. Two types of body, both in aluminium for lightness, were offered: the Sportsman sedan and the Ace roadster, both illustrated. In the latter, the rumble seat was entered via the front seat. There were four forward speeds, with direct drive on third gear and an overdrive on top gear. Maximum speed on the latter was in excess of 100 m.p.h. The Speedway Eight, an extremely expensive departure from Jordan tradition, was the company's last gasp.

38 MG 18/100 TIGRESS,
1930, Great Britain

The MG Tigress, a sports-racing car in the classic British mould, was the most highly developed version of the 2½-litre six-cylinder MG fast tourer introduced in 1928. This, in turn, was based on the new overhead-camshaft Morris Six of 1928, thus following the normal MG recipe of the time, which was to take the current Morris touring car, with its low cost, reliability, and availability of service and parts, and give it slightly better handling and performance, a far more elegant body, and a higher price. The formula was highly successful, appealing to the ordinary citizen who wanted to cut a dash. Cecil Kimber of the Morris Garages in Oxford (hence the name MG) had put the first of the line into production in 1924, using the side-valve Morris Oxford as his starting-point. The new MG of 1929, called the 18/80 MG Six Sports, had a Morris-based, if much modified engine, though many other parts were bought out. All the smoothness of the Morris was there, and was appreciated by its fundamentally non-sporting buyer, but the Morris three-speed gearbox was retained. To cope with this drawback, the 18/80 Mark II was introduced for 1930, the older car being renamed the Mark I and still sold. The Mark II had a stiffer, wider frame, a four-speed gear-box, better brakes, and more non-Morris parts. The result was a heavier, if better-handling car, and many people preferred the Mark I, especially in its Speed Model form, when it was offered with a narrow, light body, some with an outside hand-brake, and a guaranteed maximum speed of 80 m.p.h. This car weighed only 22¾ cwt. complete. The 18/80, as four-passenger tourer, coupé, and sedan, was made until 1932. The 18/100 h.p. Tigress, or Mark III, was a very different proposition, intended primarily for serious, long-distance road racing. For reliability, it was not too light or highly stressed, but the engine had a four-bearing crankshaft, balanced reciprocating parts, dry-sump lubrication, and twin-coil ignition. Only five were made, to a very high standard. The single body style was the four-passenger one demanded by international sports-car regulations, chassis weight being 22¼ cwt., and maximum speed was between 95 and 100 m.p.h. Although offered as a 1931 model, most were made in 1930. The model was short-lived, mainly because of the success of the MG Midget in racing (39), but it is doubtful if the Tigress could have competed seriously with lighter, faster machinery such as the supercharged 6C 17/50 Alfa-Romeo (42).

39 MG M MIDGET, DOUBLE TWELVE MIDGET, 1930, Great Britain

1928 saw the introduction of the Morris Minor into William Morris's range of popular cars and June of the same year brought its metamorphosis, in the then-customary MG way, into a sports car for the masses. The same coil-ignition, two-bearing overhead-camshaft engine, mildly tuned, the same three-speed gear-box and the same chassis were used, with lowered suspension, but the body was a very pretty two-passenger affair in plywood over an ash frame, covered in fabric, with cycle-type wings, a pointed tail, and a metal hood. Later cars had all-metal bodies. The weight was barely half a ton, and power output was 20 b.h.p., so the widely-spaced gears in fact gave quite good acceleration up to 25 m.p.h. in low gear, 45 m.p.h. in second, and 65 in top, on the 4·89 : 1 final drive ratio. The cruising speed was 50 m.p.h., which was as high as that of touring cars of three times the cylinder capacity, and hill-climbing was exceptional for so small a car. So was flexibility: it would creep along at 5 m.p.h. in top gear. By the standards of the day if not by our own, the Midget held the road well, and had good brakes. The importance of the Midget lay in its being the first really cheap, practical British sports car for the ordinary man anxious to cut a sporting image. Earlier recipes had either been too stark, like the sporting derivations of the minimal cycle-car of the early 1920s, or too expensive, like the French imports—Amilcar, Salmson, and the rest. The Midget offered modest comfort (in comparison with the first category), and low price and universal availability of parts and service (as compared with the second). The price in 1929 was only £175, sinking to £165 in 1932, the last year of production. Its thirst was very modest, at 38 m.p.g. One way and another, it was not surprising that well over 3000 were made, and that in its first full year of production, the number built exceeded that of all MGs to date. A closed coupé was also offered. Power was boosted to 27 b.h.p., and from 1931, the options of a four-speed gear-box and a supercharger were offered. The regular competition Mid-

get was the 'Double Twelve' type as shown in the lower illustration. It owed its name to the class victory of a team of special Midgets in the 1930 Double 12-hour Race at Brooklands; an event which was the nearest thing allowed by British law and public opinion to the Le Mans 24-hour Race. All the team cars finished; a tribute to their inherent reliability. The Double Twelve had the 27 b.h.p. engine, a folding windshield, an undershield, cutaway doors, a hood strap, and a larger fuel tank. Eighteen of these cars, rated at 8/45 h.p. instead of the normal car's 8/33 h.p., were made. In the touring range, the M was supplemented for 1932 by the D, with four-passenger touring and sedan bodies, while the competition Midget was developed into the formidable little C-type or Montlhéry Midget, a pure sports-racing car available supercharged or (with two carburettors) non-supercharged, powered by a hand-built, tuned, short-stroke engine inside the 750-c.c. class limit, giving 60 b.h.p. blown, at 6300 r.p.m. Maximum speed of this 13-cwt. car was 90 m.p.h.; a speed rendered usable by a stiffer chassis, greatly improved brakes, and a four-speed gear-box. In 1931 the C-type won the Brooklands Double 12-hour Race outright, the Ulster Tourist Trophy Race, and the Irish Grand Prix, but it was the old M-type, with the help of the competition successes of all models, that started a trend and made Britain the leader in the cheap sports-car field. Needless to say, in the U.S.A. at this time, it was regarded as a joke, though one was displayed at the New York Automobile Show in 1930, and Edsel Ford was a buyer.

40 INVICTA 4½-LITRE TYPE S, 1930, Great Britain

Few cars can have had a more promisingly sporting parentage than the Invicta. Noel Macklin had been responsible for the Eric-Campbell and its derivative the Silver Hawk, both machines for the sportsman rather than the family man in spite of their plebeian origins, while J. G. Parry-Thomas, Macklin's consulting engineer, designed the luxurious but advanced Leyland Eight, the Leyland-Thomas racing car that grew from it, the Marlborough-Thomas of 1923 and the Brooklands Riley (27), both the latter being very fierce little cars indeed. However, the Invicta itself when it appeared in 1925 was not initially a sports car, but a new type designed to combine American flexibility, reliability, and durability with British handling and quality. The result was a high, unhandsome but expensive touring car with a six-cylinder Meadows engine of 2·7 litres (from 1926 enlarged to a capacity of 3 litres), that was remarkable only for its extreme tractability and ruggedness. The former quality was evinced by its ability to stay in top gear from a walking-pace to 60 m.p.h., and the latter by well-publicized long-distance endurance runs by the Cordery sisters. But in 1928 there came a shift in emphasis, towards high performance. A new 4½-litre dual-ignition engine, again by Meadows, was installed in the 3-litre chassis. This gave 85 m.p.h. and notably good acceleration. In 1929 the frame was stiffened up. This model NLC, a formidable fast tourer, not yet a sports car, was supplemented in late 1930 by the sensational S-type Invicta (see illustration). Noel Macklin had come back to a true sports machine in every sense. The chassis was shorter than that of the NLC, and was lowered by flattening and underslinging the rear springs. The radiator, too, was lower, giving the whole car a very rakish and businesslike air. The weight of the open model with the normal short two/four-passenger body, was 28½ cwt., and it usually pulled a 3·6 : 1 axle ratio. The speed range in top gear was 6–95 m.p.h., with over 75 m.p.h. available in third gear, and 60 m.p.h. coming up in under fifteen seconds from rest. The S-type's common nickname '100 m.p.h.' was never an official designation, and was misleading as far as production cars were concerned. The power output in standard form was 102 b.h.p., but Raymond Mays and Peter Berthon, later associated with E.R.A., working with Murray Jamieson who was responsible for the later twin overhead-camshaft racing Austins, developed an S-type to give 158 b.h.p., still at a very modest 3900 r.p.m. Steering, brakes, and roadholding were first class, though oversteer set in during high-speed cornering, The open tourer was the normal style, but coachbuilt coupés were also seen. About fifty S-types were made in all, from 1930 to 1935. A plan to replace it with the fabulous SS-type, with 5-litre, twin overhead-camshaft supercharged engine and five-speed Wilson pre-selector gear-box, came to nothing. The S-type distinguished itself in road events rather than racing. Driven by Donald Healey, one gained a clean sheet in the 1930 International Alpine Trial. The S-type won the 1931

Monte Carlo Rally and was second in 1932, in Healey's hands, and in these years again had clean sheets in the Alpine Trials, winning Coupes des Glaciers: that is, they lost no penalty points.

41 OM 2·2-LITRE, 1930, Italy

The OM Type 665 (14) the best-known car made by the Officine Meccaniche of Brescia, had great endurance as well as a surprising turn of speed (for a side-valve-engined car) in its more exciting forms, but it was basically a fast tourer, not a sports car, and in competition it could not compare with the 75 b.h.p. of the Alfa-Romeo 6C 1500 (see 42). Attempts were made in both Britain and Italy to make the OM go faster. L. C. Rawlence, the British agents, made six cars with an overhead-valve cylinder-head and 85 b.h.p. In Italy, the side-valve car was Roots-supercharged to give 80 b.h.p., lowered by means of under-slung springs, lightened to 17 cwt., and given a distinctive raked radiator. It was still not fast enough to hold the Alfa-Romeos, so in 1929 the engine was enlarged to 2·2 litres by means of a bigger bore, and given a finned cylinder-head. Coil ignition was standard, but dual ignition by coil and magneto could be had. This unit provided 55 b.h.p. unblown, and 85 b.h.p. blown. A handful of still fiercer works team cars appeared in 1930. They had 2350 c.c. (67 × 110 mm.) engines, supercharged in all cases, producing 95 b.h.p. at 4000 r.p.m., still from a side-valve engine. This 2·3S was never put into production. Indeed, the last OM passenger cars were made

around 1931, after which only commercial and public service vehicles were built.

42 ALFA-ROMEO 6C 1750 GS, 1930, 1933, Italy

The Alfa-Romeo 6C of 1926 was a new departure for the Milan firm, famous already for large-engined fast-touring machines in the classic mould that had made their mark in competitions. The designer Vittorio Jano introduced his firm to the idea of a practical all-purpose car with a small but highly efficient engine, of modern design, providing an excellent power-to-weight ratio, in a chassis with good handling characteristics. The engine was of only $1\frac{1}{2}$ litres' cubic capacity, compared with the 3 litres of the standard Alfa-Romeo to that date, yet it combined an output of over 43 b.h.p. with dependability and smooth and flexible running. The unit had an overhead camshaft and was made mostly of aluminium. It was employed for the first couple of years mainly to pull large sedan bodies with the help of low axle ratios, but in 1928 the obvious step was taken, and the first sporting model appeared. In it, low weight was added to the 6C's other virtues. The combination was formidable. This car still had the 1500 c.c. engine, but with two overhead camshafts. The sports type developed 53·5 b.h.p. unsupercharged, and 75 b.h.p. in Super Sport form, with Roots-type blower. The latter type won the Spa 24-hour Race and the Mille Miglia in the year of its introduction, the Brooklands Double 12-hour Race in 1929, and a second place in the 1929 Ulster Tourist Trophy

Race. In the first half of 1928, fractionally more Normale or touring models with the single camshaft were made than sports cars, but the emphasis was changing. The ultimate development of the 6C 1500 arrived in 1929, with the 6C 1750, which had a slightly larger bore and longer stroke. It superseded the 1½-litre type, carrying on the options of single overhead camshaft unblown, and twin o.h.c. supercharged or unsupercharged models. Power output varied from the 46 b.h.p. of the first-named to the 84 b.h.p. of the blown Super Sport, and the 102 b.h.p. of the fabulous Gran Sport Corsa, of which a handful were made in 1930. The SS or Super Sport, in later series (from 1930) called the GS or Gran Sport, was capable of 90 m.p.h. The range was extended in 1931 by a twin o.h.c. supercharged touring version, giving 80 b.h.p., and completed in 1932 by the little-known 1900 GT model, with 68 mm. bore, 1920 c.c., and two overhead camshafts, providing 68 b.h.p. The last-named was a car of different, less sporting concept, with its synchromesh gear-box and free wheel. The classic type was undoubtedly the Super Sport and Gran Sport, with its beautiful, lean and hungry Zagato-designed bodies, introduced on the 6C 1500 and pioneers of a fashion. Reliable high performance with low weight and fine handling was an alliance which the old type of sports car, exemplified by the Bentley and S-type Mercedes-Benz (25, 17) could not defeat. The 6C 1750 won the Mille Miglia in 1929 and 1930, and was second in 1931. It won the Spa 24-hour Race in 1929 and 1930, coming in second in 1931, the Irish Grand Prix in 1929, and the Ulster Tourist Trophy Race in 1930. A second place was gained in the 1931 Targa Florio. The victories of 1930 and later were due to the Scuderia Ferrari, who ran the works team Alfa-Romeos from then until 1937. The whole range was withdrawn in 1934, after 2591 6C 1750s had been made and the company had gone into liquidation, through making cars that had a too-limited market.

43 MERCEDES-BENZ 370S MANNHEIM SPORT, 1931, Germany

The first range of cars produced by the recently-constituted Daimler-Benz A.G. in 1926, and called Mercedes-Benz, included two completely new models. These were extremely hard-wearing, modern machines on conventional American lines, offering low-priced space, comfort, durability, and flexibility of running, at the expense of conservative power outputs, weight, and low and gappy gearing. Both were side-valve sixes with three speeds and servo-assisted brakes. The smaller was the 2-litre Stuttgart, and the larger the 3-litre Mannheim, rated at 12/55 P.S., and giving the indicated 55 b.h.p. With its flat radiator in contrast with the hitherto universal Mercedes vee, and its artillery-type wheels, it was a vehicle of uninspiring aspect as well as performance, which performed its modest task well. It became the Mannheim 350 in 1928, with 3·4 litres and 60 b.h.p., and was further enlarged a year later as the Mannheim 370, of 3·7 litres, four forward speeds, and 75 b.h.p., developed at 3100 r.p.m. This was a car of fine quality, that had progressed beyond its rather plebeian origin. The Mannheim 370S Sport, which appeared in 1930 and was made until 1932, seems to have used the same engine, installed in a lower chassis wearing much more elegant bodywork. In fact, it was one of the best-looking cars of an age of handsome machines, though it was heavy, at rather under 30 cwt., and so could not exceed 75 m.p.h.

44 STUTZ DV32 BEARCAT, 1931–5, U.S.A.

The Stutz Vertical-Eight introduced in 1926 (3) was one of the finest big, high-grade, high-priced cars on the American market, but by the end of the decade the power output of its single overhead-camshaft engine in normal form—115 b.h.p.—had been surpassed by the latest offerings of Cadillac, Packard, Pierce-Arrow, and Auburn (66) aimed at the same market, while further competition was coming from Marmon, Franklin, and Lincoln. More power was needed, so at the end of 1930 a new cylinder-head was offered on a new model alongside the old. It had twice as many chain-driven overhead camshafts and valves as the existing car; hence the name DV32—Dual Valve (two inlet and two exhaust per cylinder); thirty-two valves in all. The design, by Charles Greuter, begetter of the Vertical-Eight, was inspired by that of the Model J Duesenberg (78), but simplified. Power output was 156 b.h.p. at 3900 r.p.m. The DV32 Stutz was running in prototype form in 1930, and in production in the spring of the following year. Seventeen body styles could be had on the normal chassis,

which was good for over 90 m.p.h. The famous old name of Bearcat, used previously for the most exciting Stutz models, was revived for the new speedster. Two variations were offered: the 42-cwt. Bearcat Torpedo Speedster, a four-passenger car with cutaway doors and rounded tail, and the 35-cwt. Super Bearcat. The latter was sold on the short, 9 ft. 8 in. wheelbase instead of the 11 ft. 2½ in. length. Both cars were guaranteed to exceed 100 m.p.h. In fact the Super Bearcat would reach 105 m.p.h. in top and 70 m.p.h. in third gear. In 1932 a three-speed synchromesh gear-box was substituted for the less-popular, more 'European' four-speed 'crash' box, which was not as retrograde a step as it sounds, since the new gear-box had better-spaced ratios than the old. 1933 was the last year of production, and the last DV32 was sold in 1935. With the DV32, Stutz continued their determined efforts in international competitions, initiated in the 1928 Le Mans 24-hour Race, in which a Vertical-Eight came in second and almost defeated Britain's Bentleys, and pursued in the 1929 event. Edouard Brisson, who had driven Stutzes on these occasions, handled the new DV32 in 1930, 1931, and 1932, though with no success. The DV32-engined Stutz Special was more successful, making fastest time of the day in the Pike's Peak hill-climb in 1932, 1933, and 1934.

45 DELAGE D8SS, 1931–5, France

Until the arrival in 1930 of the first Delage D8, the firm had made only one entry into the luxury field, with the

GL or Grande Luxe six-cylinder model of 1924–8, a vast 6-litre machine quite unlike the much more famous fours and sixes that were Delage's bread and butter; high-quality middle-class cars all. The Lory-designed D8 combined the refinement and comfort of a prestige car with distinctly sporting habits. Claimed power output varied between 90 and 120 b.h.p. at 3400 r.p.m., but this was well within the engine's capabilities, providing performance without high stresses. Maximum speed was between 80 and 87 m.p.h., depending on the body and length of chassis used. Even the 'short' chassis had a wheelbase of 10 ft. 10 in., but it was extremely rigid, the servo brakes were excellent, the steering was very fine, and the D8 could be handled like a sports car. The 35-cwt. sports sedan on the short chassis (D8C—*court*, short) pulled the highest alternative axle ratio of 3·9 : 1, but could still trickle down to 6 m.p.h. in top gear, and offered greater refinement than its predecessor, the six-cylinder DMS. The D8 attracted some very fine, if sometimes over-blown bodies, too—by Letourneur et Marchand, Vanden Plas, Figoni et Falaschi, Van Vooren, and other famous names. It must have seemed like gilding the lily when, in 1931, the frame was dropped, and a still more exotic motor-car appeared on it—the D8SS or Grand Sport. This vehicle, the model illustrated, was developed from the D8C, and had a raised compression ratio, the D8 series' valve gear with the springs operating separate rocker-arms to avoid valve bounce, a high-lift camshaft and a guaranteed maximum speed of 100 m.p.h. from 145 b.h.p. at 4500 r.p.m., on the 3·6 : 1 axle ratio. This model excelled at high-speed endurance tests, the prototype taking the 24 hours record to 109 m.p.h. at Montlhéry in 1931, and in 1932 averaging 112 m.p.h. for 12 hours. A few D8SS were imported into Britain with four carburettors. The D8 series was continued until 1935 with the D8SS, the D8S or more ordinary sports model, and the D8N or Normale. Alongside the aristocrats, there were offered in great profusion a variety of sixes and fours, some fine cars, others lamentable descents into the cheap and nasty utterly unworthy of the name of Delage. In 1935 the company was taken over by Delahaye (79), and henceforth the eight-cylinder Delage was the superb Delahaye Type 135 with two more cylinders—thus the new D8100 of 1936, and its sports alternative, the D8120. However, the most distinguished of the Delahaye-built Delage sports models was the new D6/70 six-cylinder, 2·7-litre of 1937, which derived from an earlier Delage six, and had a Cotal electric gear-box, three carburettors, and independent front suspension by transverse leaf springs and wishbones. The fixed-head coupé was quite exceptionally pretty. The D6/70, unlike the D8, was developed as a competition car, coming in fourth in the 1937 Le Mans 24-hour Race and second in 1939, and winning the 1938 Ulster Tourist Trophy Race. In the 1949 Le Mans 24-hour Race, a D63L, the development of the D6/70, came in second and won its class. The engine now produced 142 b.h.p. at 5300 r.p.m.

46, 47 DERBY L2 6CV and 1500, 1931–4, France

From 1921, when the firm began manufacture, until the end of the decade the Derby from Courbevoie (later St Denis) was best known as a conventional little car with a predominantly sporting image; a typical assembled French *voiturette* of the time, in fact. By the later 1920s, however, this type was dead; the ordinary motorist was demanding more comfort and refinement. A line of good, small C.I.M.E.-engined sixes was the last new offering of the 1920s, intended to fit the mood of the time. However, after new management had taken over, in 1931 there arrived a completely new and highly unusual chassis designed by Lépicard, who had been responsible for racing cars of the Donnet concern. The advanced specification embraced front-wheel drive by an 1100 c.c. 6CV Ruby engine (from 1933), or a 2-litre, 11CV V8 engine of Lépicard's design. The first was the L2 model, and the second the L8. The ingenious independent suspension was by pivoted forked arms and a transverse leaf spring at front and rear. At the front, the arms were hollow, allowing the drive shafts to pass through them. Steering was by split trackrod, pivoted in the centre. The Ruby-engined car produced 35 b.h.p., and pulled a 4·1 : 1 axle ratio. The chassis weighed less than 11 cwt., but was long enough to allow exceptionally roomy bodywork. The Derby-built V8 was interesting as to its engine, also, this having overhead exhaust and side inlet valves. The Derby was quite well known in Britain, since the agent was Vernon Balls, the energetic promoter of small French sports cars, and Mr W. D. Hawkes was manager of the Paris works. Mrs Hawkes (Gwenda Stewart) won publicity for the name at Montlhéry and Brooklands with her special Derby-Miller record-breaker and her Derby-Maserati circuit car. Three front-drive production chassis were fitted in Britain with the $1\frac{1}{2}$-litre Meadows overhead-valve engine, and were called the 1500. The last Derbys were made in 1936.

48 ALVIS 12/60, 1931–2, Great Britain

When the Alvis 12/50, on which the fortunes of the company had been built, was dropped at the end of 1929 in favour of the six-cylinder Silver Eagle and front wheel-drive sports car (13), the famous Coventry concern found themselves without a cheaper, more popular model. Thus the 12/50 was hastily reintroduced late in 1930, with a new type designation, TJ instead of TG, justified by some minor modifications: mainly coil ignition as a standard fitting, with a magneto optional, a crankshaft vibration damper, a wider frame, and improved brakes. The gearchange was right-hand, to a separate gear-box, in the traditional British manner. This was strictly a touring car, with the choice of two- or four-passenger open bodies, or sedans. Then, in March 1931, a new two-passenger sports version was introduced to replace the SD sports model of 1929. This, designated the TK 12/60, was a fine all-rounder, the last development of a basically sound, conventional design. Two carburettors were fitted instead of one on the TJ and the gear ratios were closer, though retaining the final drive ratio of 4·77 : 1. The engine produced 52 b.h.p. and though the complete car weighed $21\frac{1}{4}$ cwt., it showed 65 m.p.h. in third gear and up to 75 m.p.h. in top, together with very good brakes and an economical fuel consumption of 28 m.p.g. Detail improvements were introduced in the TL 12/60 of 1932, but though the model was catalogued for 1933, it had gone by then. Alvis had made their last true sports car.

49 **TALBOT 105,** 1931–7, Great Britain

Up to the middle 1920s, Clement Talbot Ltd, a British member of the Anglo-French Sunbeam-Talbot-Darracq combine, were making big, old-fashioned touring cars and expensive small cars extremely well, in very small numbers. They also made, in 1924–5, a fine, more modern small-six, but in even smaller quantities. The company was sliding downhill, and Georges Roesch, its talented Swiss designer, had to do something quickly. His aim, daringly, was to provide the refinement, speed and space of the Rolls-Royce Twenty at half the price, engine size and weight. The result was his 14/45 Talbot, introduced at the 1926 Olympia Motor Show. This very modern car had a small but highly efficient six-cylinder engine of 1665 c.c. (61 × 95 mm.) utilizing a high-compression ratio, and extremely light valve gear of Roesche's own, very clever design. There was coil ignition, which was itself quite unusual at this time in Britain. This engine produced

41 b.h.p. at 4500 r.p.m., which (with the help of a low axle ratio) sufficed to propel a long, heavy, rigid frame loaded with a spacious body at up to 65 m.p.h. Particularly after it had undergone improvements at the end of 1928, the new Talbot's combination of virtues made it a rousing success. This revised, better-braked 14/45 had the potentiality in it of a faster car, and early in 1930 two new models were introduced beside the 14/45. The basis of both was a bigger engine of 2276 c.c. (69·5 × 100 mm.) with seven main bearings instead of four and larger valves, providing 60 (later 76) b.h.p. The new type, the Talbot 75, in $33\frac{1}{2}$-cwt. sedan form in 1936 could reach 78 m.p.h. in top gear and 52 m.p.h. in third. Roadholding was very good. Meanwhile, during 1930 Fox & Nicholl, the Talbot dealers, interested in competitions, instigated the insertion of the 75 engine, with a higher compression ratio and 80–85 b.h.p., still at 4500 r.p.m., in the new short 14/45 Scout chassis, and the clothing of this potentially very exciting chassis in a light fabric four-passenger body with pointed tail and cycle-type wings. Cars of this type won their class in Irish Grand Prix, Ulster Tourist Trophy Race, Brooklands 500-mile Race and Le Mans 24-hour Race of 1930, impressing all with their combination of silent, smooth running and extremely high speed, unheard-of in sports cars. Their performance in the 1930 Le Mans Race was particularly sensational, finishing as they did third and fourth behind two Speed Six Bentleys (25). The sports type was sold as the Brooklands 90, but Talbot 90 sedans and tourers were also made. Fox & Nicholls' next move

was to enlarge the engine still further, to take full advantage of the 3-litre class limit, the new engine's 75 × 112 mm. bore and stroke making 2969 c.c. The main design change lay in valve gear that was reliable at high speeds. The racing engines gave between 118 and 138 b.h.p. This allowed a class win in the 1931 Brooklands Double 12-hour Race and the Irish Grand Prix, a second place in the 500-mile Race, and a third place at Le Mans in 1932. The production car, called the 105, had a 100 b.h.p. engine. The 105 had a fine record in the International Alpine Trial as well as in races. It lost no marks in the 1931 event, and won the team prize in 1932 and 1934. The works Alpine cars in the latter year carried light four-passenger bodies and cycle-type wings, giving a weight of $29\frac{1}{4}$ cwt., and had 126 b.h.p. engines that provided just short of 100 m.p.h. in top gear with a 0–70 acceleration time of 19 seconds. The 1933 sedan was capable of 88 m.p.h. For that year, a Wilson pre-selector gear-box was offered as an option. It became a standard fitting. The final development of this superb and versatile design was the Talbot 110 of 1936, which had a centrifugal clutch and the 105 engine with a bigger bore of 80 mm., giving 3377 c.c. By this time Clement-Talbot Ltd was in the hands of the Rootes brothers and were no longer racing officially, but a competition car with tuned 110 engine gave 164 b.h.p. at 4800 r.p.m. The normal engine developed 123 b.h.p. at 4500 r.p.m., which was enough to drive the $32\frac{1}{2}$-cwt. tourer pulling a 4·3 : 1 axle at 90 m.p.h., and to offer a 0–60 acceleration figure of 15·4 seconds. In 1938 the 110 was

dropped, and the Roesch Talbots were no more. Of the much longer-lived 105, around 700 examples were made.

50 MASERATI 8C-1100, 1931, Italy

Of the six Maserati brothers, five were at various times involved in the Italian motor industry. From 1922, Alfieri, who had made spark plugs, developed the Diatto car for competitions. When Diatto gave up racing, Alfieri and some of his brothers brought out the first cars bearing their own name from their Bologna works, starting in 1926. The cars of the Officine Alfieri Maserati were all competition machines. Until after the Second World War, they were almost all racing cars, in many cases adaptable enough to be used in sports-car racing, and were sold to the public for all types of contest. This was made easier by the fact that until 1933, when Maserati made their first *monoposto* racing car, all their machines had two-passenger bodies. It was only in 1932 that this type had ceased to be compulsory in Grand Prix racing. The first Maserati was the Tipo 26, a $1\frac{1}{2}$-litre machine intended for local Italian competition. By 1930, three cars were being made; the 8C 2500 with 175 b.h.p. at 6000 r.p.m., which took part in road trim in the Irish Grand Prix and Ulster Tourist Trophy races of 1931, coming second in the former with a four-passenger body; the 8C 1500, which was an improved (shorter, more substantial) Tipo 26, with 120 b.h.p.; and the 8C 1100, which won its class, suitably road-equipped, in the 1931 and 1932 Mille Miglia. Its engine gave 100 b.h.p. at

5500 r.p.m., which with a weight of under 16 cwt. gave a maximum speed of 115 m.p.h. All three cars were offered in sports trim if required. All used the basic two overhead-camshaft, straight-eight engine with Roots-type super-charger, aluminium pistons, tubular connecting rods, and two valves per cylinder. In 1934, a four-cylinder 1100 c.c. Maserati was also sold, the 4CTR 1100, a lighter car (little over 12 cwt.) with 105 b.h.p. which won its class in the 1934, 1935 and 1936 Mille Miglia.

51 ALFA-ROMEO 8C 2300 MONZA, 1931–3, Italy

Between 1931 and 1934, Alfa-Romeo built a series of cars that were the ultimate development of the famous Jano-designed 6C series (42). It is not quite true to say simply that the 8C was the 6C 1750 with two cylinders added, since the new engine was in two blocks of four cylinders, with a ten-bearing crankshaft. This expensive, complex car, difficult to maintain, had come far from the original 6C design, but it retained the 6C 1750's cylinder dimensions and general technical features. Detail differences included dry-sump lubrication and supercharging on all the eight-cylinder machines. The 207 examples made came in three models. The fiercest was the Monza, illustrated. This was a pure sports-racing car (used, indeed, as a Grand Prix car under the Formula Libre until, and after, the introduction of the P3—see below). It was equally at home with road equipment or stripped. It gained its name from its win in Campari's hands in the

Grand Prix of Europe at Monza in 1931. It was seen on the shortest, 8 ft. 8 in. wheelbase, with magneto instead of coil ignition, higher com-pression ratio, larger valves, different camshaft, and a higher-pressure super-charger. This recipe, with 3·7 or 3·9 : 1 axle ratio, produced 178 b.h.p. at 5400 r.p.m. and 130 m.p.h. In 1933 the Scuderia Ferrari, who by then were racing outside the control of the Milan works, enlarged the bore of their Monzas to 68 mm. and the cubic capacity to 2557 c.c. The Mille Miglia-type 8C 2300 had a 9 ft. wheelbase, a 4·25 : 1 axle ratio, and a maximum of 110 m.p.h., while the Le Mans, on the long, 10 ft. 2 in. chassis, wore a four-passenger body to suit the rules of the Le Mans 24-hour Race, but still weighed only 19½ cwt., and had an engine developing 153 b.h.p. at 5200 r.p.m., which gave it a clear 115 m.p.h. maximum speed on the 4·5 : 1 axle. The 8C 2300 was the most successful and versatile Alfa-Romeo of all time. Its triumphs included, apart from the first Monza win, victories in the 1931 Belgian Grand Prix, and in the 1932 Mille Miglia, Monaco Grand Prix, Targa Florio, Eifelrennen, and 24-hour races at Le Mans and Spa. The 1933 list was longer: it comprised wins in the Mille Miglia, Tunis Grand Prix, Targa Florio, Tripoli Grand Prix and Eifel-rennen, and again at Le Mans and Spa. As late as 1934, a 2·6 Monza won the Mille Miglia again, and a 2·3 was vic-torious at Le Mans. These achievements, be it noted, were to the credit of two-passenger cars; the deeds of the mono-posto pure Grand Prix car of 1932, the Type B P3, are outside the scope of this book.

52 BUGATTI TYPE 55,
1932, France

Ettore Bugatti's sports cars evolved from his racing cars in the classic manner. Just as the ferocious Type 43 sports machine of 1927 (10) was basically the Type 35B Grand Prix car detuned, so the 43's successor, the Type 55, had evolved in 1932 from the Type 35's phenomenally successful supplanter, the Type 51 blown Grand Prix car of 1931. This Type 51 was the first racing Bugatti to use the new twin overhead-camshaft cylinder-head with two inclined valves per cylinder (said to be influenced by the American racing designer Harry Miller) rather than the former single-camshaft, three-valves-per-cylinder layout. This engine, with a lowered compression ratio and developing 135 b.h.p. at 5000 r.p.m., was installed in the immensely strong chassis that had been used for the unsuccessful 4·9-litre Type 54 Grand Prix car, also of 1931, that had been too fast for its drivers. A variety of axle ratios was to be had, from 3·37 : 1 to 3·9 : 1. The supremely elegant standard two-passenger sports car had a body designed by Jean Bugatti, with cutaway sides and long, flared wings. The complete car weighed only 22 cwt. Not surprisingly, performance was well up to Bugatti standards. Maximum speed was up to 115 m.p.h., with 100 m.p.h. available in third gear and acceleration times of 8·7 seconds for 0–50, 13 seconds for 0–60, and 43 seconds for 0–100 m.p.h. Handling, too, was as to be expected. At the same time, the Type 55 was a more refined machine than the old Type 43, reflecting changing taste in being well sprung and more comfortable, and in having a less rough and noisy gear-box, and an easier clutch—although the gear-change was still tricky. The driving position was upright in the contemporary Grand Prix manner, rather than prone in the normal sports-car manner of the time. Cast alloy wheels, as fitted to Bugatti Grand Prix cars, were used.

53 LAGONDA TWO-LITRE,
1928–1932, Great Britain

Until 1925, the Lagonda was known as a small economy car, technically more interesting than most, but intended for the family man of modest means. This was the quite popular 11 h.p. machine. Then there came a complete change of policy. The 14/60 h.p. Sports Tourer Lagonda introduced in August 1925 was a fast tourer on the lines of the H.E. (26) and the long-legged mile-eaters from famous French factories such as Delage (9) and O.M. (14). Its engine, while being extremely reliable, was of advanced specification, producing 60 b.h.p. at 4200 r.p.m. and 65 m.p.h., with 53 m.p.h. available on the third gear of the pleasantly close-ratio gear-box. At the same time, fuel consumption was a modest 25 m.p.g., the car was designed for simple maintenance, and a combination of flexibility, light steering, and easy gear-change belied the rakish sporting appearance of the four-passenger tourer. Sedans were also offered. In 1927 came the more famous, and still more desirable Speed Model on the same chassis. Its engine was set further back, the compression ratio was higher, and the gear ratios were even better chosen, 80 m.p.h.

coming up in top and 70 m.p.h. in third. The best-known version of the Speed Model came in 1929, with lowered frame and cycle-type wings. Though the car had never been designed as an out-and-out sports model, it was progressing in that direction. Its weight now told against it; gearing was too high for the weight and for the power available. In 1931, therefore, came the supercharged Speed Model, with Cozette blower, 85 b.h.p., 90 m.p.h. in top and 80 in third, at the expense of the prized Lagonda virtue of dependability. The unblown car was continued, its last manifestation being the Continental of 1932 (lower illustration), distinguished by a sloping radiator. No more Two-Litres were made after that year.

54 ALVIS SA SPEED TWENTY, 1932–3, Great Britain

Towards the end of 1931, the Alvis company produced the prototype of what was a completely new type of car for them; a big machine intended for fast long-distance touring, with its emphasis on speed, refinement, space and elegance. There was much about the Speed Twenty of 1932 that was traditionally Alvis—notably the combination of better-than-average performance and handling with character and quality, and also the $2\frac{1}{2}$-litre, six-cylinder engine, which was a development of that already being used in the 20 h.p. Silver Eagle model; but the rakish, glamorous, luxurious lines, redolent of expense in what was in fact the cheapest car of its class on the

market, and the unit construction of engine and gear-box, were novelties to the firm. Three carburettors and a dual ignition system by coil and magneto were fitted. The car was not light—few in this class were—but in spite of a weight of 26 cwt. for the open tourer, a maximum speed of between 85 and 90 m.p.h. was obtainable on the 4·55 : 1 final drive, with between 60 and 70 available in third gear, together with a fuel consumption of 18 m.p.g. Power output was 87 b.h.p. at 4200 r.p.m. The most normal body styles were sports tourers and sedans, all of them designed by coachbuilders: Vanden Plas, Charlesworth and Cross & Ellis. A few of the type shown at the bottom of the page, the Cross & Ellis two-passenger model, were also made. From 1934, Alvis emphasis was less on the Speed Twenty's sporting character and more on its truer nature as a fast tourer. Weight went up, and complication set in, in the form of transverse-leaf independent front suspension, and an all-synchromesh gear-box (Britain's first). A larger engine logically followed in 1935, and 1936 was the model's last year. It was replaced by the Speed Twenty-five for 1937.

55 WOLSELEY HORNET SPECIAL, 1932, 1933, Great Britain

In late 1930, Sir William Morris introduced the Wolseley Hornet touring car as a six-cylinder version of the Morris Minor, with two extra cylinders of the same dimensions, a longer chassis-frame, Lockheed hydraulic brakes, and the Morris' three-speed gear-box. The Hornet was intended as a small, cheap six of the then-fashionable type, but improved upon most of the breed in its good power-to-weight ratio—the result of a lively overhead-camshaft engine in a light chassis—its relatively high axle ratio of 4·78 : 1 and its brakes. The new car offered a surer basis for a cheap sports car than most of its type. The first to see this were outsiders such as Eustace Watkins Ltd, Wolseley London agents, and Colonel Michael McEvoy, who specialized in high-performance tuning. Both used the standard Hornet chassis at first, the latter producing the more businesslike machine, with improved breathing, oversize rear tyres, lighter body and outside hand-brake; while the former, fitting bodies made by Abbey, concentrated on providing sporting appearance for the ordinary mortal who wanted to cut a dash. Then, in 1932, Wolseley themselves produced a sports chassis, the Hornet Special, which they sold bare, for the customer to fit one of the multiplicity of bodies offered by Eustace Watkins, Swallow (see illustration, bottom), Jensen (Avon), and the rest of the specialized coach-builders who flourished at this time by making sporting bodies and minor mechanical alterations for cheap mass-produced cars. The Hornet Special chassis specification included a 40 b.h.p. engine with twin carburettors, special manifolding, alloy high-compression pistons, alloy connecting-rods, double valve springs, and an oil cooler; a pleasant remote-control gear-box with four speeds; twelve-inch brakes; a wider front track to improve the poor steering-lock and roadholding, and a lowered axle ratio

of 4·89 : 1—this to take advantage of the 5000 r.p.m. now available, and to encourage competition in the sporting trials becoming ever more popular in Britain. Maximum speed of a Hornet Special with two-passenger 'Daytona' body by Eustace Watkins (see illustration, top) was 70 m.p.h., with 58 m.p.h. available in third gear. It would accelerate from a standstill to 50 m.p.h. in 17·8 seconds, which was not really very startling. McEvoy, for his part, again built a more serious competition car, with supercharger and stiffened frame at the front. The 0–60 figure was 12·8 seconds. The 1934 Hornet Special chassis was itself improved, with a longer wheel-base, underslung frame at the rear, and a 47 b.h.p. engine that had better breathing, yet was smoother. Top speed was around 75 m.p.h. In the following year, a 14-h.p. Hornet Special was introduced beside the old 12 h.p. With a slightly enlarged bore and stroke, 1604 c.c. and 50 b.h.p., maximum speed was about the same as for the latest 12 h.p., but was achieved with fewer revolutions and greater reliability. By 1936, however, both types had gone out of production; as in the case of the MG (58, 59, 60), which was part of the same empire, policy had changed away from a sporting bias. Not that Wolseley, unlike MG, ever raced the Hornet Special; this was left to private interests

56 ASTON MARTIN LE MANS, 1933–4, Great Britain

The new Aston Martin sports car that appeared late in 1927 was the result of the fusion of two lines of design.

Augustus Cesare Bertelli, a Briton of Italian descent who had been riding mechanic to the great Felice Nazzaro, had developed the somewhat pedestrian Enfield-Allday for competition work, then with W. S. Renwick had designed and made one car, basically Enfield-Allday but with his own special overhead-camshaft cylinder-head. Meanwhile, the firm of Bamford & Martin, taking its name from Robert Bamford and Lionel Martin, had been making a small and conventional but very fine, very expensive sports car, the Aston Martin, in extremely small numbers. In 1926 the firm was reconstituted as Aston Martin Motors Ltd with Bertelli in charge of design. The new Aston Martin of 1927 was more modern, complex and solidly built than its predecessor, but was equally well made. The $1\frac{1}{2}$-litre engine used Bertelli's overhead-camshaft head with inclined valves, the camshaft being chain driven. Lubrication of the first few cars was of the conventional wet-sump type. There were four forward speeds in a separate gear-box, an underslung worm-driven rear axle, and a very low, stiffly-sprung chassis. The new car was sold in normal and short, two-carburettor form, in which guise the engine developed 64 b.h.p. In 1929 the company entered motor sport seriously with a new model, the International Sports, which first made its name. This car differed from its forerunner in having dry-sump lubrication, and less weight to carry—but at $19\frac{1}{2}$ cwt. the normal round-tail open two-four-passenger model was still too heavy. Even weightier sedan and coupé bodies were also listed. There was a pleasant close-ratio gear-box and an

axle ratio of 4·75 : 1. Power output was 56 b.h.p. at 4500 r.p.m., and maximum speed around 80 m.p.h. In 1930 a more powerful engine giving an 85 m.p.h. top speed was offered as an alternative. The ultimate development of the International was also the first Aston Martin to make a serious mark in motor sport. These 1931 works-team cars had 70 b.h.p. engines, weighed 17 cwt., and could exceed 90 m.p.h. They won their class in that year's Le Mans 24-hour Race, Ulster Tourist Trophy Race, and Brooklands Double 12-hour Race—all the long, gruelling events in which the heavy but strong Astons always excelled, and in which stamina was more important than acceleration and outright maximum speed. From this model the Le Mans model Aston Martin was developed, for 1933, as the successor of the International. It was a cheaper car, with unit construction of engine and gear-box and a bevel axle, lower-geared and lighter steering. Not quite so uncompromising as the stock International, it was slightly higher-geared, and a lighter, faster, and better car. Weight was 19 cwt., and guaranteed maximum 84 m.p.h. Externally, it was recognizable by its outside exhaust system and its slab fuel tank at the rear. Even the four-passenger sports tourer, which weighed $22\frac{1}{2}$ cwt., and pulled the long, 10-foot chassis instead of the short, 8 ft. 6 in. option, was capable of 80 m.p.h. The Le Mans model was modified slightly in 1934 as the Mark II. In the same year the finest of the Bertelli cars made its bow, the Ulster model. This was an out-and-out sports-racing car, of which only a score or so were built. The engine used a higher compression ratio and a high-

lift camshaft giving 80 b.h.p. at 5250
r.p.m. The standard long-tailed two-
passenger model weighed under 18
cwt., and was guaranteed to reach
100 m.p.h. The last year of the $1\frac{1}{2}$-litre
Aston Martins was 1935; thereafter, a
new design took over (81). In their
time, they had had a remarkable run of
racing successes, of which the most
famous were the 1931 wins already
mentioned, further class wins at Le
Mans in 1932, 1933, 1935 and 1937,
the team prize in the Tourist Trophy in
1934 and 1935, and class wins in the
1935 Mille Miglia and 1936 24-hour
Race at Spa. Subsequently, the now-
obsolete car did well in French hands in
the Bol d'Or 24-hour Race, winning
its class in 1938 in V. A. Polledry's
hands and winning the event outright
in 1939, driven by M. Contet.

57 LAGONDA RAPIER,
1933–6, Great Britain

With the $4\frac{1}{2}$-litre M45 Lagonda of
1933, the company introduced their
first small car for many years, but one
in the same semi-sporting tradition as
its bigger brothers. A beautifully-made
little twin-o.h.c. engine produced 46
b.h.p. at 4500 r.p.m., and would rev up
to 6000 r.p.m. It needed all its power,
for it was expected to pull a heavy
body, usually a convertible or a closed
style. Four-passenger tourers and two-
passenger sports models were also
offered. The standard gear-box was far
from light, too, being an ENV pre-
selector unit. Low gearing was needed
to cope with this weight. Still, maximum speed was 80 m.p.h. in open
form, which was highly creditable for

so small an engine, especially when one
considers the weight it had to pull. In
1936 Rapier Cars Ltd took over the
design from L. G. Motors, and offered
the car as the Rapier. W. H. Oates,
formerly of Lagonda, developed it. The
Rapier was sold supercharged or unsupercharged. Weight was $19\frac{1}{2}$ cwt.
(the open tourer), and a 5·28 : 1 axle ratio
usually fitted. Maximum speed in
blown form was 90 m.p.h. in top and
68 in third, with 60 m.p.h. coming up
in 12·6 seconds from rest. This extra-
ordinary performance for an 1100 c.c.
production car was matched by equally
remarkable smoothness.

58 MG J2 MIDGET, 1933,
Great Britain

In the development of some cars, it can
clearly be seen that racing improves the
breed. This was certainly so in the case
of MG in the 1930s. As related under
(39), the C-type or Montlhéry sports-
racing Midget incorporated many
improvements not solely concerned
with extracting more power. Some of
these were carried over into the next
generation of normal MG Midgets, the
J models of 1932–4. These had a four-
speed gear-box, a stiffer chassis, better
brakes, a cylinder-head of improved
design, and two carburettors. Power
output was now 36 b.h.p. at 5500
r.p.m., compared with 27 b.h.p.,
though the two-passenger J2 was a
heavier car than the M-type at 13 cwt.,
and the final drive ratio had gone down
to 5·375 : 1, partly to allow competition
in the cross-country trials then booming
in Britain. Maximum speed was well
over 70 m.p.h. As the J1, sedan and

four-passenger touring models were sold. In its way, the J2 was as great a trend-setter as the M-type, for it was so popular, with over 2000 units built, that it set the sports-car fashion for low build (thanks to an underslung frame), a short, remote-control gear-lever, cutaway doors, and a slab fuel tank at the rear with spare wheel mounted thereon. The J in its fiercest form was seen as the supercharged J3 and J4 cars, the latter a road racing machine. The latter was second in the 1933 Ulster T.T. Race. The J was in turn developed into the last of the classic overhead-camshaft Midgets, the P series, which had a three-bearing crankshaft (not before time), more power, better brakes, and more weight.

59 MG L MAGNA, 1933,
Great Britain

At the end of 1931, Cecil Kimber of MG took the new small six-cylinder overhead-camshaft Wolseley Hornet engine, another William Morris product that was basically the o.h.c. Morris Minor unit with two extra cylinders, and installed it, with modifications, into a sports version of the Wolseley. His theory was that there was a market for a more sporting type of Hornet, with all the refinement and flexibility of running of the six; a market that MG was about to leave empty with the demise of the 18/80 model (see 38). As usual, he was proved right. The first of the new Magna series was called the F-type. Tourers and sedans were made. Its 1271 c.c. engine developed 37 b.h.p. at 4000 r.p.m. The 15¼-cwt. four-passenger

tourer pulled a 4·78 : 1 axle ratio, and there were four forward speeds. This was a 70 m.p.h. car. The F2, the two-passenger sports car of 1932, had bigger brakes. The F series was developed into the L series of 1933, which was designed to fit into a competition category not yet covered by MG: the 1100 c.c. class (though here again, tourers and sedan versions were offered). The 1087 c.c. engine of the two-passenger sports car, the L2 Magna, was smaller than that of the F Magna but was more efficient, developing 41 b.h.p. at 5500 r.p.m. The L2 was half a hundredweight heavier than the F, too, and the axle ratio was lower. The company and private individuals used the L2 for racing on the Brooklands track, and it won the team award in the 1933 Alpine Trial. To the Magnas, late in 1932, was added the more substantial Magnette range (see 60).

60 MG K3 MAGNETTE,
1933–4, Great Britain

For 1933, the L Magna range of MGs was supplemented by the larger, wider, heavier Magnettes whose chassis were designed primarily to carry four-passenger bodies. However, the K1 Magnette was developed for competition purposes into the superb K3 Magnette, an almost entirely conventional but remarkably successful road-racing six-cylinder machine. A prototype took part in the 1932 Monte Carlo Rally, but the model first made its mark in the 1933 Mille Miglia Race, when three cars took part and one won the 1100 c.c. class, defeating the considerably more specialized Maseratis (50). The engine dimensions were unchanged from the L-type, but a Powerplus supercharger car produced 120 b.h.p. at 6500 r.p.m. On production cars, there was the choice of a Wilson pre-selector gear-box, or a normal manual change. Magneto ignition was used instead of the Magna's coil, and there was a straight-cut bevel final drive. Partly because of the Wilson box, and mostly because of the Magnette series' general solidity of construction, the K3 was a heavy car, at $18\frac{1}{4}$ cwt., but it could exceed 110 m.p.h. The 1934 model had the slightly less potent but more reliable Marshall supercharger, and was lighter at $17\frac{3}{4}$ cwt. In 1933 customers were offered the choice of a long pointed tail or a slab-tank tail, but few of the former was sold until 1934. About 30 K3s were built, and won a sporting reputation out of all proportion to their numbers. Apart from their class win in the 1933 Mille Miglia, they won (in the hands of Raffaele Cecchini) the Coppa Acerbo Junior and the Italian 1100 c.c. championship in that year and 1934, the Brooklands 500-mile Race and the Ulster Tourist Trophy Race of 1933, their class in the Le Mans 24-hour Race in 1934 and 1935, driven by Maillard-Brune, and the classic Bol d'Or Race in 1938 and 1939. Another K3 was developed as the special EX135, a notable breaker of international class records. Beside the K3 was a range of normal sporting machines, the K1 sedan and the K2 two-passenger open car. They were superseded in 1934 by the 1286 c.c. N-type Magnettes, which were current until 1936. One of these, the NE roadracer, developed to meet a ban on

supercharging, won the 1934 Ulster Tourist Trophy Race.

61 **VALE SPECIAL,**
1933–6, Great Britain

Numerous small-scale assemblers of cheap sports cars sprang into existence in the early 1930s, in response to the market revealed by MG (39), and died as suddenly. One of the better known was the Vale Engineering Company, which in 1933 expanded its tuning activities into car manufacture. The Vale Special was a more businesslike sporting machine than most of its kind. It started with a good basis: the current Triumph Super-Eight engine, a reliable side-valve Coventry Climax unit with a three-bearing crankshaft capable of speeds of up to 6000 r.p.m. It was set in an extremely short frame of 7 ft. wheelbase, with the track-rod and steering-box ahead of the front axle. The centre of gravity was very low, thanks to a frame underslung at front and rear, and underslung worm final drive. As a result, this was an exceptionally stable little car, and with its hydraulic brakes, an unexpected refinement, it stopped very well. A variety of gear ratios could be had, and the final drive ratios offered were 5·25 or 5·75 : 1. Accessibility of the mechanical components was first class; a feature to appeal to the new generation of sporting motorists. In 1934, when Triumph went over to an engine layout incorporating overhead inlet and side exhaust valves, Vale followed suit. Three types were offered, in the original wheelbase with 5·25 : 1 axle: there were two four-cylinder units of 1100 and

1500 c.c., and a 1500 c.c. six-cylinder. When it was powered by the latter two engines, the Vale Special could attain 90 m.p.h. In all, a little over 100 Vale Specials were built between 1933 and 1936. One was a single-seater racing car made for Ian Connell. This has the 1500 c.c. four-cylinder engine supercharged and producing 97 b.h.p. at 5700 r.p.m. Its maximum speed was a remarkable 125–130 m.p.h. Replicas were offered for sale, but none was made.

62 WIKOV SPORT,
1933, Czechoslovakia

Wichterle & Kovarik, agricultural machinery manufacturers and foundry-men, made their first car in 1922. Like most successful Czech car builders, they concentrated on small machines for the leaner pocket. Typically, too, the latter were technically of unusual interest. Their standard offering in 1929, when they went into serious production, was a 1-litre family machine that grew in size over the years to two litres. The basis of the most successful sports Wikov was the $1\frac{1}{2}$-litre model. Its engine was a unit of advanced specification, providing around 30 b.h.p. The overhead-camshaft layout with inclined valves allowed well-shaped combustion chambers. The block was of aluminium, with steel liners. Pistons and connecting-rods were of alloy, and the crankshaft was balanced. The Sport version had a short chassis with a 9-ft. wheelbase, dropped front axle, crab-tracked front wheels, high-geared steering, an iron cylinder-block (surprisingly) with steel liners, and stronger, hollow steel connecting-rods. This was a very fast little car (85 m.p.h. unsupercharged, over 100 m.p.h. blown) but possessed of great stamina, which was necessary for success in the gruelling Czech long-distance high-speed trials of the period, such as the High Tatra International Rally, covering two weeks or more. The Wikov Sport also had notable wins in Czech and Polish races. The fastest examples were fitted with streamlined bodies designed by Jaray, whose coachwork was seen on Tatra and Jawa cars, and on German makes such as Dixi as well. The biggest, a 2-litre production car, with a 10-mm. larger bore, produced 43 b.h.p. It was a comfortable fast tourer, with centra-lized chassis lubrication. Manufacture ceased in 1937.

63 SQUIRE, 1934–6,
Great Britain

Among dedicated enthusiasts of the true sports car, the name of Adrian Morgan Squire is among the immortals, on the strength of exactly ten cars made, between 1934 and 1939. Squire's was a sports car made in the classic mould; its design was conventional, in that it would refine normal practice rather than offer startlingly advanced design. Made to an ideal, the Squire was naturally very expensive. Its engine was the extremely noisy, if powerful R1 Anzani unit with two gear-driven over-head-camshafts, a gear-driven super-charger, twin water pumps, and oil-cooler. Power output ranged up to 110 b.h.p. at 5000 r.p.m. With a 3·6 : 1 axle ratio, this gave the short-chassis two-passenger car a guaranteed maximum speed of 100 m.p.h., with 76 m.p.h. available in third gear, and the remarkable acceleration time of 15 seconds from rest to 70 m.p.h. in spite of the Wilson pre-selector gear-box. There was also a four-passenger model on a longer chassis. The roadholding, aided by a very rigid frame and thermostatically controlled shock-absorbers, was superb. The Squire looked the part, with its most elegant raked radiator and swept wings. A cheaper version, the so-called 'Skimpy' with cycle-type wings and starker body, was not as handsome. Only seven cars of both types were built by Squire. When he went out of business in 1936, a customer, Val Zethrin, took over the components that remained and put together three more cars between 1937 and 1939.

64 BENTLEY 3½-LITRE,
1934, Great Britain

The market for big, expensive, complicated sports and luxury cars on traditional lines shrivelled away in the Great Depression of the early 1930s, and Bentley Motors went into liquidation in 1931. Walter Owen Bentley left, Rolls-Royce gained control, and in 1933 Bentley Motors (1931) Ltd announced their first car. A lot of abortive experiment was behind it. Initially, Rolls-Royce had planned the new Bentley as another sports car of the fiercer sort, called the Peregrine, with their existing 20/25 h.p. Rolls engine scaled down to 2·3 litres and supercharged, installed in a new chassis. In the end, the 20/25 engine itself, modified for higher per-

formance in respect of two carburettors, an altered induction manifold, and a higher compression ratio was fitted to the Peregrine chassis. It was mated with a gear-box with close ratios that was pleasant to use, a 4·1 : 1 (or 3·9 : 1) final drive ratio, very good servo-assisted brakes, and light steering. The outcome was a car that combined sports-car performance and handling with great refinement and complete tractability; a rare alliance of virtues in the days when sports cars as a class were noisy, draughty, and sometimes temperamental. Bentley called it their 'Silent Sports Car'. Power output was 110 b.h.p. at 4500 r.p.m. 90 m.p.h. was to be seen in top gear and 75 in third, and the cruising speed was anything up to 80 m.p.h. The weight of the convertible by Park Ward was 32½ cwt., but fuel consumption was very moderate. At steady speeds, 20 m.p.g. or better was common. Roadholding was improved in 1934 by stiffening the front of the frame, and at the same time automatic ride-control (shock-absorber adjustment) was introduced. In spring 1936, a bigger, 4¼-litre engine was introduced. This provided better acceleration. The Rolls-produced Bentley was a machine designed for stamina at continuous high-speed cruising velocities, not for racing, but its adaptability extended beyond normal road work. With a special two-passenger sports-bodied 3½-litre (see lower illustration), and works support, E. R. Hall came home second in the Ulster Tourist Trophy Races of 1934, 1935 and 1936, on the last occasion with a 4¼-litre engine. Even his 3½-litre engine could be developed to give 152 b.h.p. with complete reliability.

65 FIAT TIPO 508S, 1934, 1935, Italy

In 1932, suffering like everyone else from the Great Depression, Fiat abolished their existing range and introduced a cheaper, more modern line to attract the widest possible market, from the Tipo 522 of $2\frac{1}{2}$ litres at the top end to the Tipo 508 small car at the bottom. The latter was a completely new design. Although a solid, stolid little car of unexciting specification, it was ahead of its time in its class in having a short-stroke engine, which allowed high engine speeds without high piston speeds, thus producing the quite high output of 22 b.h.p. from less than a litre of side-valve engine. This in turn helped to permit the relatively high axle ratio of 5·2 : 1, which meant that the 508 could cruise at up to 55 m.p.h., although its maximum speed fell short of 60 m.p.h. The brakes were hydraulically operated. The car merited its type name of Balilla—'plucky little one'. Not surprisingly, some 80,000 were built. Nor was it surprising that this promising chassis was developed into a fine sports car. The 508S of 1933, weighing only 12 cwt., had a mildly tuned engine giving 30 b.h.p., and a light, simple, elegant two-passenger body (with its flared wings and vestigial dorsal fin) very reminiscent of some sporting versions of the earlier Tipo 509 and Tipo 514 small cars (which were in turn 'cribbed' from the classic Zagato shapes on the Alfa-Romeo). The cars that took part in the 1933 Mille Miglia Race had overhead-valve cylinder heads and four-speed gear-boxes. These improvements were carried over into the second series 508S (or, correctly, 508CS). This was now a truly notable machine, with 60 m.p.h. available in the third gear of the close-ratio box, and 75 m.p.h. in top. Power output was 36 b.h.p. at 4000 r.p.m. A top gear ratio of 4·3 : 1 permitted high cruising speeds, and a 32 m.p.g. fuel consumption. A few of the Coppa d'Oro variant, with a lighter, even starker body, were made. One special 508S developed 48 b.h.p. in supercharged form, weighed only half a ton, and on a 4 : 1 axle could reach 96 m.p.h. Better known was the remarkable Berlinetta Aerodinamica coupé of 1935. An aerodynamic body was also seen on the new 1100 c.c. 508C chassis of 1937, with independent front suspension and a tubular backbone frame. This extremely advanced little *gran turismo* coupé combined a 90 m.p.h. maximum and 80 m.p.h. cruising with a fuel consumption of 40 m.p.g. at 60 m.p.h., thanks to its good shape, special 3·5 : 1 axle ratio and 42 b.h.p. engine. The 508S, meanwhile, had been raced in Simca form by Amedée Gordini. Simcas won their class in the 1936 French Grand Prix (for sports cars), Bol d'Or Race, and Spa 24-hour Race. The Fiat version won its class in the same year's Ulster Tourist Trophy Race. Class wins in the 1937 Mille Miglia and Le Mans races followed, for Fiat and Gordini. In Germany, the 508S was made as the N.S.U.-Fiat. In all, around 900 were built of the Italian version alone.

66 AUBURN MODEL 851 SPEEDSTER, 1935, U.S.A.

The Auburn Speedster of 1935–6 was the last of a distinguished line of exceptionally attractive sport cars in the American idiom. The first production Auburn, named after its town of origin in Indiana, saw the light in 1903, but it was a little-known make until 1919, when the Beauty Six was introduced. This was a medium-quality six with a Continental engine, already an unusually handsome car. However, the company went into decline until 1924, when Errett Lobban Cord became general manager, and later President. He transformed the Auburn fortunes, not by technical changes, but by revolutionary styling, pioneering the long, low look in an age of sit-up-and-beg sedans and sawn-off tourers in the modest price range. The new Auburn's combination of elegance and low price was prophetic of Jaguar policy of ten years later (98). This 8/88 of 1926 had, like all succeeding Auburns, a side-valve engine made by Lycoming Motors, acquired by Cord in 1927. The reliable, durable eight-in-line unit developed around 70 b.h.p. at 3200 r.p.m. In 1928 the first two-passenger speedster of the new series arrived, with higher compression ratio and axle ratio, and modified suspension. At the same period, the engine was improved. This 8/115 and its successor the 8/120 produced 115 b.h.p. at 3300 r.p.m. In turn, the 8/125 of 1930 gave the indicated power at 3600 r.p.m. Small wheels in 1927 accentuated the low lines of the car, and a much stiffer frame was introduced in the same year. Cord was a believer in rigid frames, which on the Auburn were progressively stiffened up. Internal expanding Lockheed hydraulic brakes were fitted.

The eight-cylinder Auburns of 1931–3 incorporated economies and were much cheaper than, but otherwise basically similar to, their predecessors. They had a freewheel, and from 1932 a Columbia two-speed axle, giving an optional high final drive ratio of $3·47 : 1$, was adopted. The Auburn eights were supplemented from 1932 by the fabulous V-12, a low-priced twelve-cylinder car with the refinements of a machine in the luxury price bracket, and intended to replace the L-29 Cord (21). However, the V-12 was dropped from 1934, and the eight was given a fractionally larger bore, which was now as in the car illustrated. This 850 series arose from the arrival at Auburn of Gordon Buehrig and August Duesenberg, respectively the chief body designer and chief engineer of Duesenberg Inc., which with Cord and Auburn formed the Cord Corporation. Their plan was to combine an inexpensive, reliable supercharger installation in the tried eight-cylinder chassis, to provide a prestige successor to the V-12. Power output of the Model 850 and 851 engine was 115 b.h.p. at 3600 r.p.m., increased to 148 b.h.p. at 3900 r.p.m. when supercharged. Six body styles of supercharged car were listed, from a limousine to the Buehrig-styled speedster. The two-speed axle was standard on the supercharged cars and optional on the rest. The speedster was only offered in supercharged form. The maximum speed of the latter was 100 m.p.h. In spite of being supercharged, the speedster's engine was notably smooth, flexible and quiet. This fine car died in the collapse of the Cord Corporation in 1937.

67 FRAZER NASH T.T. REPLICA, 1935, Great Britain

The chain-driven Frazer Nash of 1924–38 was a highly individual assembled sports car that carved a niche for itself by sheer force of personality. Its fierce acceleration (thanks to an excellent power-to-weight ratio), fine roadholding, simplicity, strength, and moderate price outweighed the unorthodoxy of chain drive (a separate chain for each forward speed), dog-clutch gear-change, solid rear axle, very direct steering, simple bodywork and unyielding quarter-elliptic suspension. These characteristics stemmed from its cycle-car ancestry, in the shape of the elementary but effective GN that had been made by H. R. Godfrey and A. Frazer-Nash. In the Frazer Nash, made by the latter alone, there were four cylinders instead of two, but, at first, still only three forward speeds. H. J. Aldington took over from Frazer-Nash in 1929. He was later joined by his brother. The side-valve Anzani engine was dropped in favour of the more powerful overhead-valve Meadows unit. A bigger, heavier, roomier body (though still a cramped two seater with outside gear and brake levers and single door) was devised, and with this and the Meadows engine, a new model was born—the T.T. Replica of 1932, so called after the car entered in the 1931 Ulster Tourist Trophy Race. The standard 55 b.h.p. engine in the $17\frac{1}{2}$-cwt. car provided 85 m.p.h. and an 0–50 acceleration time of 10 seconds. Up to 100 m.p.h. could be seen with special tuning. Albert Gough, one of the company's engineers, developed the deflector cylinder-head, which with higher compression ratio and larger valves produced 62 b.h.p. from the engine at the same revolutions—4500. More than half of the T.T. Replicas made had the Meadows engine; some used more expensive, heavier, rather less reliable if more powerful overhead-camshaft engines—either the Gough-designed single overhead-camshaft unit with 60 b.h.p., as in the car illustrated, or the proprietary double overhead-camshaft Blackburne six-cylinder engine (supplied by an outside manufacturer) which gave an output of 70 b.h.p. at 5000 r.p.m. The Blackburne-engined cars weighed 2 cwt. more than the rest, but combined an 87 m.p.h. maximum with smoothness and refinement hitherto foreign to the Frazer Nash. This unit was used in the Colmore model, the most civilized variant. It was available (and most usually seen) in 1667 c.c. form, but with a bore reduction, could be brought into the $1\frac{1}{2}$-litre competition class. Fifty-four out of 85 T.T. Replicas made had the Meadows engine. These 85 cars formed the mainstay of the make from 1932; an indication of how a modest concern could keep afloat with tiny production runs. The T.T. Replica did extraordinarily well in club competition, but its only international success was in the Alpine Trials of 1932, 1933 and 1934, in each of which cars came home without loss of marks (four out of six entered in the last year mentioned).

68 RILEY IMP, 1935, Great Britain

At the end of 1933, Riley Ltd introduced a new sports model on their ultra-successful 9 h.p. chassis to replace the Brooklands (11). In fact it was a different concept, being altogether less fierce, more practical for general use, and far better-looking. The Imp, with its long flared wings and long hood (mostly toolbox—not much of it engine), was one of the most elegant sports cars of the 1930s—which was not surprising, as its style was an obvious copy of the beautiful Zagato bodies of contemporary and earlier Alfa-Romeos (42). Underneath was some rather more prosaic machinery—the Nine chassis with wheelbase shortened to 7 ft. 6 in., the optional Special Series Nine engine with two carburettors, a higher compression ratio, 5000 r.p.m., and 41 b.h.p., and the normal Nine gear-box. A Wilson pre-selector box was available on request. The axle ratio was low, if typical of the period: 5·25 : 1. Maximum speed was a clear 70 m.p.h., which was not exceptional, but at 17 cwt. this was not a light car. The smaller-engined, cheaper MG J2 Midget (58) would do better, with less power. The Imp was dropped in 1935. However, a variation called the Ulster Imp, made in very small numbers, was a different proposition. It had a still higher compression ratio (8·25 : 1), a crankshaft with detachable balance weights, and a final drive ratio of 4·77 : 1.

69 TRIUMPH GLORIA SOUTHERN CROSS, 1935, Great Britain

Donald Healey, who became famous after the Second World War for the fine sports cars bearing his own name,

was until 1939 in charge of design at the Triumph Motor Company. He was responsible for the new Gloria range introduced in 1933 which were fast, modern semi-sporting cars with chassis underslung at the rear, rather than family machines. They were available in four- or six-cylinder form at different times, all engines being the familiar Coventry-Climax unit with overhead inlet and side exhaust valves. The three-bearing four was at first a 1087 c.c. unit developing 40 b.h.p. at 4000 r.p.m., but it was soon supplemented by the 1232 c.c., 42 b.h.p. engine. The latter was tuned for use in the Gloria Vitesse, the Speed Model and its successor, the Monte Carlo sports tourer, and the full sports car for 1935, the two-passenger Gloria Southern Cross. Two carburettors, high-lift camshaft, polished ports, and stronger valve springs were used in the last-named, whose engine developed 50 b.h.p. at 4750 r.p.m. The car was intended as an inexpensive all-rounder; solid, well-built (weighing 18½ cwt.), but was also a serious competition car. The gear-box had wide ratios and acceleration was sluggish, 28 seconds being needed to reach 60 m.p.h. in sedan form, but a freewheel was provided, the low-speed torque was excellent, the maximum was over 70 m.p.h., and the happy cruising speed was anything up to 60 m.p.h., so clearly this was a car intended for easy top-gear motoring rather than fierce getaways. Road-holding was very good. The Gloria Vitesse and Gloria Southern Cross were also to be had in six-cylinder form. The latter, with 1·8-litre, 70 b.h.p. engine, was said to have a performance equal to that of the 15/98 h.p. Aston Martin

(81). After 1936, Triumph concentrated on fast prestige cars with less of a sporting image, but not before Donald Healey had won his class and was third overall in the 1934 Monte Carlo Rally.

70 MARENDAZ SPECIAL 15/98 h.p., 1935–6, Great Britain

Captain D. M. K. Marendaz made the Marseal light car until 1925, then turned to assembling a characterful sports car which he called the Marendaz Special. Then, as later, it was an exceptionally low, good-looking car, with a very Bentley-like radiator. Into the same chassis were fitted, to choice, a $1\frac{1}{2}$-litre side-valve Anzani engine, rated at 11/55 h.p. (or 11/120 h.p. supercharged), or an 1100 c.c. overhead-valve unit of 9/20 h.p. These cars made their name by taking class records on the Montlhéry circuit. In 1932 there arrived, in deference to fashion, a small 2-litre side-valve six, the 13/70 h.p. (13/90 h.p. supercharged), parts of which engine were possibly of American, Continental manufacture, modified and put together by Marendaz. There was also a bigger, 2·6-litre machine, the 17/90 h.p. (17/100 h.p. supercharged). All these cars had excellent hydraulic brakes. The most successful Marendaz was undoubtedly the new 2-litre six of 1935, illustrated here. This 15/98 h.p., which had a fully-floating rear axle, used an overhead-inlet, side-exhaust valve engine made by Coventry-Climax, available blown or unblown, in the customary Marendaz fashion. It was distinguished by outside exhaust pipes, and maintained the make's reputation for dashing good

looks. In normal form the car was capable of over 80 m.p.h., with acceleration figures of 10·6 seconds for 0–50, and 15·8 seconds for 0–60 m.p.h., combined with great tractability. Mrs Alfred Moss, mother of Stirling Moss, drove a specially prepared 15/98 successfully in competitions (see upper illustration). Production ended in 1936.

71 AUSTIN SEVEN NIPPY, 1934–8, and SPEEDY, 1934–5, Great Britain

The Austin Motor Company had offered a mildly sporting variant of its renowned Seven as early as 1924, but it was little known, and its much more famous successor, the Super Sports introduced in 1928 and renamed the Ulster in 1931 (13), was a stark sports-racing machine that made no concessions to the wide market that existed for cheap sports cars beyond the handful of competition drivers. This market was recognized, and catered for, by innumerable specialist body-builders and tuners such as E. C. Gordon England, Boyd-Carpenter, and Swallow. However, by about 1933 all but a few of these had disappeared, or stopped modifying Austin Sevens, leaving a gap to be filled. The Ulster was no longer made; its appeal was too specialized. The best known of Austin's answers for the ordinary man anxious for a sporting exterior was the Nippy. It started life as the '65' model in 1933, to be renamed the following year. It was powered by a special unit with high-compression cylinder-head, high-lift camshaft, downdraught carburettor, and a large-finned sump. Power output was 23 b.h.p. at 4800 r.p.m., providing 65 m.p.h. The front spring was stiffened up with binding, and the front axle was dropped. There was a close-ratio gear-box. This was not a specially fast car, but in 1936 it was fitted with the slightly more powerful, fully pressure-fed engine that had been supplied with the ephemeral '75' or Speedy of 1934–5, one of which is illustrated in the lower painting. Alongside this new Nippy was one with a standard engine, which by now (1936) had three bearings and an output of 17 b.h.p. It seems that at least one Nippy, that illustrated with outside exhaust pipes, was super-charged for export to the U.S.A. Another variant on the Nippy chassis appeared in 1937, though not as a production car, when the works entered the Le Mans 24-hour Race. These cars were derived from the 'Grasshopper' works-trials machines of 1934–7. They were very fierce indeed, with engines capable of turning at 7000 r.p.m., and maxima in top and third gears of 80 and 60 m.p.h. Some were supercharged. Low-chassis versions were built for road racing. They ran at Le Mans with unsupercharged, Murray Jamieson-modified engines and door-less bodies, while the cars entered in the Tourist Trophy Race, also in 1937, were supercharged.

72 RAILTON LIGHT SPORTS TOURER,
1935–6, Great Britain

Serious production of the Invicta (40) had ceased by 1933, and its manu-facturer, Noel Macklin, had been look-ing about for a substitute of similar character, offering the same combina-tion of low-stressed engine, simplicity, exceptional power-to-weight ratio and low-speed torque, and good handling. The formula Macklin chose was an American chassis with a lightly tuned engine, somewhat improved roadhold-ing and lighter bodies. He utilized the Hudson range; first the eight-cylinder Essex unit and then (in 1934) the Hudson eight, both of around four litres' capacity. The basic Hudson three-speed gear-box with synchromesh between top and second was fitted. The engine was tuned mildly, by means of a raised compression ratio, to give 124 b.h.p. at 4000 r.p.m. instead of the Hudson's normal 113 b.h.p. at 3800 r.p.m. Friction shock-absorbers helped to make the Railton safe at speed. Otherwise, the chassis was Hudson. Even the sedans were capable of 90 m.p.h. The standard four-passenger tourer weighed no more than 21–2 cwt. The few modifications to the Hudson were carried out by Reid Railton, who had helped design such high-per-formance machines as the Brooklands Riley (27). Weight went up as time passed. In 1936 Hudson hydraulic brakes were adopted. By far the most formidable Railton, and the one least akin to its Hudson parentage, was that illustrated. The Light Sports Tourer, of which only three were made weighed only 19½ cwt., with its short (9 ft. 8 in.) wheelbase and doorless alloy body with cutaway sides and cycle-type wings. The handbrake was outside. The steer-ing was higher geared than normal. Maximum speed on the 3·6 : 1 axle ratio was 100 m.p.h., with 70 m.p.h. available in second gear. For a road car, the acceleration was remarkable, 50, 60,

and 70 m.p.h. coming up in 7, 9·8 and
13·6 seconds from rest. The top-gear
step-away was even more astonishing.
10–30 occupied two seconds, and 20–40
2·8 seconds. The 1935 prototype had
been capable of 107 m.p.h., with 80
m.p.h. in second and a 0–60 acceleration time of 8·8 seconds. Even faster
special versions were built. Yet with it,
the Light Sports Tourer was tractable
in the Railton tradition.

73, 74 BSA THREE-WHEELER, and SCOUT, 1935, 1936–9, Great Britain

The pedigree of what was one of
Britain's more interesting cheap sporting cars went back to 1929, when the
motor-cycle division of the Birming-
ham Small Arms Company introduced
a competitor for the Morgan (14), in
the shape of a technically more
advanced machine, a three-wheeler
designed by F. W. Hulse, with independent front suspension and front-
wheel drive. The engine was a 1-litre
air-cooled vee-twin with aluminium
crankcase and pistons and iron cylinder-
liners, originally made by Hotchkiss of
Coventry, that had been fitted in a
slightly different size to the BSA light
car of 1922–4, and had subsequently
been bought by BSA when Hotchkiss
were taken over by William Morris.
A four-wheeled version with a dead
rear-axle was made in 1932, and in the
following year the basic machine
developed in two directions, a 1075 c.c.
four-cylinder engine being offered in
the three-wheeler, and the same engine
going into a 'proper' four-wheeled

chassis with live axle but the same
system of front-wheel drive and
independent suspension. The two-
passenger Scout version of the latter,
with bored-out 1204 c.c. engine was
first offered in 1936. This was not a
sports car in the sense of a machine suitable for serious competitions, but was
intended, like so many others of its kind,
for the ordinary man who wanted to
look like a sportsman. It was better-
looking and technically more sophisticated than most of the breed, and
handled comparatively well. The engine
was reliable, but though available with
two carburettors, was not capable of
much development, for the crankshaft
had only two main bearings. Power
output was 26 b.h.p. The engine was
made in unit with the gear-box. The
last series of Scout was a better car, with
three-bearing, 32 b.h.p. engine that
gave the little machine a 70 m.p.h.
maximum on the 5·2 : 1 axle ratio. It
was made until 1939.

75 BMW TYPE 328, 1936–40, Germany

The Type 328 BMW was the ultimate
development of the distinguished series
of highly efficient, modern cars designed by Fritz Fiedler that had begun
in 1933 (92). It combined the rigid
tubular frame and independent front
suspension of the earlier sports models
of the line with a new and greatly
improved cylinder-head. Other BMWs
had had a normal pushrod-operated
overhead-valve head. On the 328, the
single low camshaft operated the inlet
valves normally through pushrods and
rockers, but from the rocker-shaft on

one side transverse pushrods drove further rockers on the other side of the head, operating the exhaust valves. This design allowed an excellent combustion-chamber shape and inclined valves without recourse to two overhead camshafts. The outcome was 80 b.h.p. and 95 m.p.h. for the $16\frac{1}{2}$-cwt, car in normal trim, with 3·7 : 1 axle, with 120 m.p.h. available when modifications supplied by the makers were fitted—special camshafts, pistons, carburettors, ignition, and gear ratios. lighter reciprocating parts, etc. The Type 328 BMW was one of the most successful sports cars of all time. It retained, or greatly improved upon, the performance, roadholding, precision of control, power-to-weight ratio, tractability, reasonable price, economy, and comfort of the whole series, and was of excitingly modern appearance, with its flush wings, headlamps, and hood. There were hydraulic brakes. An aluminium two-passenger sports body was the normal style, but cabriolets and convertibles by Wendler were also offered. Factory team cars included some special aerodynamic machines such as the 1940 Mille Miglia cars. Four hundred and sixty-two of the 328 were made in all, between 1936 and 1940. Such an unprecedented combination of virtues rendered the car unbeatable in its class: it was a general-purpose sports car that regularly defeated stark, stripped sports-racing machinery of the traditional type without effort, with full road equipment in position. The 328's more important victories included class wins in the 1936 and 1937 Tourist Trophy Races, a class win and team prize in the 1938 Mille Miglia, outright victory in the 1940 Mille Miglia or Brescia Grand

Prix, a class win at Le Mans in 1939, in the Grand Prix des Frontières at Chimay in 1937, 1938, and 1939, in the Nurburgring and Eifel races in 1936, in the 1938 Avusrennen and German Grand Prix, and in the 1938 Spa 24-hour Race. Indeed, the roll of victories went on after the Second World War, culminating in a class win in the International Alpine Trial as late as 1952. This is not surprising, since the Type 328 was not obsolete. It can still hold its own on the road. The 328's more 'touring' equivalent, with the same cylinder dimensions, were the 50 b.h.p. 326 (of 1936–7), its successors the 320 and 321 of 1939–40, and the faster 327 of 1938, which was a shorter 326 with 55 b.h.p. engine. The 328 engine was fitted into some Type 327 sedans and convertibles, when the car was renamed the 327/28.

76, 77 ADLER TRUMPF SPORT, JUNIOR SPORT, 1936-8, 1936, Germany

During the later 1920s, Adler, like so many European manufacturers, had been known for a variety of American types of car, of no originality or performance. These were current until 1933, but a year earlier there had appeared the first of a line of radically new machines with front-wheel drive and independent suspension, designed by Hans Georg Rohr, who remained with Adler only until 1934, but whose work coloured the firm's products for the rest of its life. At first, Rohr's Adler was a small ($1\frac{1}{2}$-litre, 30 b.h.p.) family car of modest mien, lacking any sporting pretensions. Its bore was enlarged in 1934 to provide 1645 c.c. This 1·7-litre model gave a modest 38 b.h.p. at a very conservative 3800 r.p.m. Maximum speed was around 55 m.p.h. In 1936 it was joined, however, by the Sport type with 50 b.h.p. and a raised compression ratio, which could attain 75 m.p.h. In 1935–6, Adler experimented with special aerodynamic shapes on the Frankfurt–Darmstadt autobahn and on the Avus circuit, reaching speeds of 105 m.p.h. In 1937, an aerodynamic Adler annexed the 24-hour record for cars of up to two litres' capacity. The Spa 24-hour Race of 1936 saw a 1·7 litre with aerodynamic body carry off the team prize. The 'Autobahn' sports sedan was the catalogued version of these cars. Thanks to its efficient, if ugly, aerodynamic shape, a light body of aluminium panelling over a tubular steel frame that gave the complete car a weight of less than 18 cwt., a 4·1 : 1 axle ratio could be pulled and 80 m.p.h. attained. The sports coupé with 3·57 : 1 axle was good for no less than 93 m.p.h.—still with the faithful old slogging side-valve engine. The 1·7-litre Adlers entered for the 1937 Le Mans 24-hour Race had 70 b.h.p. engines and a maximum speed of well over 100 m.p.h. In 1938, a 1½-litre engined version won its class. The Trumpf was also raced with success, in normal two-passenger open-sports form, by the Adler agent in Ireland, who assembled the cars there. The car won its class in the International Alpine Trial of 1933, and shared this victory in 1934. Alongside the 1·7 litre, there was current from 1934 to 1940 the little Trumpf Junior. Power output was 25 b.h.p. at 4000 r.p.m., which gave it the same maximum as the obsolete 1½-litre

model. This car was intended as a competitor in the D.K.W. market. The Trumpf Junior Sport of 1936–8 was an open two-passenger car with a high compression alloy cylinder-head, larger valves and carburettor, and 28 b.h.p. It weighed rather under 14 cwt., and was capable of a modest 70 m.p.h. The highly successful Trumpf was made under licence by Rosengart in France, and by Imperia in Belgium.

78 DUESENBERG SJ SPEEDSTER, 1936, U.S.A.

In 1926 Errett Lobban Cord acquired the old-established firm of Duesenberg Motors, makers of famous racing cars and of the luxurious Model A passenger car. Cord, who was President of the Auburn Automobile Company and had turned a conservative, run-down make into a byword for dashing elegance at a low price (66), was a dynamic showman with a genius for the spectacular that was at the same time commercial good sense. His aim with Duesenberg was to produce the world's superlative car; the ultimate in every way, regardless of expense. The Model J of 1929, designed by Fred Duesenberg, was the result. It combined the refinement expected of American luxury cars with technical sophistication worthy of racing practice. The twin overhead-camshaft of the eight-cylinder engine was chain driven, operating four inclined valves per cylinder. Combustion chambers were hemispherical. Yet advanced though the design was, the engine was low stressed, in the interests of reliability. Power output, 265 b.h.p.

at 4250 r.p.m., was more than double that of the fiercest production models of other American manufacturers. Although a complete four-passenger open tourer weighing 46 cwt., it was said to attain 116 m.p.h. in top gear (with axle ratios of between 3·78 and 4·7 : 1) and 89 m.p.h. in second. Brakes were hydraulic. Until servo-assistance was supplied, they were heavy to operate, but the other controls were light. The low, very stiff frame was of immense length—12 ft. 9½ in. for the long chassis, 11 ft. 10½ in. for the 'short'. All bodies were custom-built, usually being ordered through Duesenberg Inc., who created designs and had them executed by famous outside coachbuilders such as Murphy, Le Baron, Derham, Rollston and Judkins. They were generally rather ponderous, if handsome, in appearance, a light rakish line being seemingly impossible to attain with such a massive car. The chief body designer was Gordon Buehrig, later responsible for the Cord 810 (93). The chassis price, like everything else about the Model J, was larger than life— $8500 (£1700) in 1929. A complete car could cost as much as $25,000 (£5000). In 1932 the Model SJ joined the J. This car had a number of modifications as standard specifications, also obtainable as extras on the J—a centrifugal supercharger, outside exhaust pipes, larger crankshaft bearings, tubular steel connecting-rods, stronger valve springs, stiffer front springs. The short chassis and the 3·78 : 1 axle ratio were normal, but two SSJ cars were made, with a 10 ft. 5 in. wheelbase and 3 : 1 axle ratio, for Gary Cooper and Clark Gable. The normal SJ engine developed 320 b.h.p. at 4750 r.p.m., which gave the four-

passenger tourer a claimed maximum speed of 129 m.p.h. with 104 m.p.h. in second gear, and (with the roadster) an acceleration time from rest to 100 m.p.h. of 17 seconds. The J and SJ were flamboyant cars, suited to wealthy seekers after public notice such as William Randolph Hearst, Tommy Manville, Elizabeth Arden and Mayor Jimmy Walker of New York. In Europe, customers included the royal families of Spain, Italy, Yugoslavia and Rumania. Prince Nicolas of Rumania entered a J in the Le Mans 24-hour Race of 1933, 1934 and 1935, without success. It lacked the nimbleness for circuit racing, although Ab Jenkins' Duesenberg Special took many long-distance records on the Bonneville Salt Flats in Utah in 1935, attaining speeds of over 160 m.p.h. Duesenberg Inc. died in 1937, with the collapse of the Cord Corporation, and the last Model J was delivered in the following year. Upwards of 470 had been made.

79 DELAHAYE TYPE 135M COMPETITION, 1936-9, France

Until 1934 Delahaye made only solid, staid, conventional cars of derivative design for the middle-class family market, and did so in considerable variety. As a result, they did not make a great impression, and by the early 1930s seemed destined for the end that, in a time of economic distress, was overtaking so many manufacturers who neither found a niche in a specialized market nor went over to a rationalized design mass-produced at a low price. In 1934, however, they took a first step towards salvation by superseding their earlier diversified range with one basic engine, varied only in the size of the bore and the number of cylinders. It was installed in long, roomy chassis that were, even so, of very rigid, boxed construction. The new range were prestige cars, a new departure for Delahaye. Designed by Jean Francois, the engine was extremely durable, with its very robust crankshaft bearings and careful attention paid to lubrication, and was capable of much development. In one direction, it was installed in Delahaye trucks. In another, which concerns us here, it was fitted in six-cylinder, 18CV form (80 × 107 mm., 3237 c.c.) into Delahaye's first sports car, which came out in 1934. In the following year, Delahaye took up competitions very seriously. One reason was national and company repute—Bugatti, France's only other international name in racing, was now concentrating on touring cars (94) and their racing cars were no longer the success they had been. The other reason was the acquisition of Delage (45) in the same year; a firm that until its withdrawal from racing in 1927, had been France's foremost sporting *marque*. The sports Delahayes took two forms. The 70 b.h.p. 18CV was developed in 1935 into the Type 135 or Coupe des Alpes model, so called after a success in that year's International Alpine Trial. This car, unaltered as to cylinder dimensions, owned to 119 b.h.p., could attain 100 m.p.h. on its 3·42 : 1 axle ratio, and took 13 seconds to reach 60 m.p.h. from rest. Steering was pleasantly high geared. Confusingly, it was also known as the 135S (for Special). The 135M or Competition, the model illustrated, joined it

in 1936. This car had a larger bore, and breathing was aided by three carburettors and separate exhaust pipes. Power output was said to be 160 b.h.p. at 4200 r.p.m. In 135MS form, with larger exhaust valves, this was a 110 m.p.h. car. The high performance of both models was obtained in spite of the heavy, luxurious, if dashing coachwork seen on all cars except the stark two-passenger sports-racing machines. The company built only chassis, farming out the bodies to outside coachbuilders, or else selling chassis for owners to make their own arrangements. With Talbot (95), Bugatti (94) and Delage once under Delahaye control, Delahaye brought France back into prominence in international motor sport. They were second, third, fourth and fifth in the 1936 French Grand Prix (a sports-car event that year). In the Le Mans 24-hour Race, after finishing fifth in 1936, they were second in 1937, and again—in Type 175 form, developed from the Type 135—in 1951. The ultimate in Delahaye competition cars was the Type 145 Grand Prix contender of 1938, with $4\frac{1}{2}$-litre vee-twelve engine and three overhead camshafts (one per bank of exhaust valves plus one for both banks of inlet valves). This car produced 238 b.h.p. It was sold in strictly limited series, in detuned form, as the Type 165 intended for sports-racing work, with half-elliptic springs at the rear instead of De Dion suspension. At the same time, more pedestrian models were offered—the 90 b.h.p., long-chassis Type 138 and the Type 148, respectively the touring versions of the 135S and 135M: also fours and sixes in other sizes. The 135S was revived after the Second World War, being replaced in 1953 by the 235M, a refinement of it akin to the 135MS. Alongside, from 1948 to 1952, was the aforementioned new Type 175, with in-line six-cylinder 4½-litre engine and independent front suspension, as the most luxurious Delahaye. The end came in 1954, with the take-over by Hotchkiss (80).

80 HOTCHKISS GRAND SPORT, 1936, France

Hotchkiss et Cie, pioneers of the so-called 'Hotchkiss drive', by which the driving torque was taken by the springs instead of by a torque tube enclosing the propeller-shaft, and adherents of right-hand drive to the end, made a variety of rather undistinguished, anonymous middle-class cars in the earlier 1920s. They found their first really popular and successful design in the AM type of 1924–8, a completely conventional but very good side-valve four. It was joined in 1926 by the overhead-valve AM2, current until 1932, and was dropped in favour of another new car, the six-cylinder AM80. This 3-litre was a truly fine machine that became a classic thanks to its combination of outstanding refinement, good turn of speed (80 m.p.h. from 70 b.h.p.), stamina, first-class brakes and suspension, and light controls. The basic design lasted the life of the company; a further 27 years—such was its excellence, in spite of its conservatism. Not until 1948 did independent suspension arrive; a feature of all the other leading French makes in the 1930s except Bugatti. Not even Hotchkiss drive was seen on most examples of the type; the cheaper torque-tube trans-

mission was used. The AM80 was developed in 1933 into the formidable 20CV, with a larger bore of 86 mm., giving 3½ litres, but otherwise similar. In normal Cabourg sedan form, the 1934 20CV (Type 620) was capable of 80 m.p.h., and could reach 50 m.p.h. from rest in 16·6 seconds. It became the Type 686 in 1936, and by that time was good for 90 m.p.h. However, these were not the sporting cars. The Paris-Nice sedan had a high-compression engine developing at first 115 b.h.p. at 3500 r.p.m., and later up to 130 b.h.p., at the expense of some of its flexibility. The complete car weighed 30 cwt., and could pull higher, closer ratios than its more sedate sister. On the 3·6 : 1 axle ratio, maximum speed was over 90 m.p.h., with a third-gear speed (and cruising speed) of 75 m.p.h. The fiercest variant was the Grand Sport, a 100 m.p.h. machine on a shorter chassis, normally seen with coupé or sedan bodies, weighing 28 cwt., and with an 0–50 acceleration time of 10 seconds. The Grand Sport was current from 1937 to 1939. A range of smaller sixes and fours accompanied the 20CV, and following the merger of Hotchkiss with Amilcar in 1937, Hotchkiss found themselves selling the unconventional Amilcar Compound, with front-wheel drive, independent suspension and unitary construction, and the equally off-beat Hotchkiss-Gregoire of 1952, both products of the fertile genius of J. A. Gregoire (22). However, the Type 686 lived on, acquiring independent front suspension, a Cotal electric gear-box, and hydraulic brakes in 1948. It survived as the 2050 from 1951 until the end of the company's car-manufacturing life in 1954. The 20CV and its developments were not out-and-out sports cars, but their other qualities helped them to an unparalleled run of successes in the Monte Carlo Rally, winning this event in 1932 (with a prototype), in 1933, 1934, and 1939, and in 1949 and 1950. The International Alpine Trial was another scene of triumph with the class team prize in 1933 and a Coupe des Glaciers in 1934.

81 ASTON MARTIN SPEED MODEL, 1936–8, Great Britain

In 1936 an entirely new range of Aston Martins was announced, replacing the Bertelli cars of 1927–35 (56). They were the outcome of a change of control, by which R. G. Sutherland took over and radically altered design policy, although the new design itself was executed by Bertelli before he left the company in 1936. The engine of the new 15/98 Aston was enlarged from $1\frac{1}{2}$ to 2 litres, reverted to wet-sump lubrication, and was made much quieter and more flexible. In keeping with this appeal to a wider, less sporting market, a synchromesh gear-box was provided, there were hydraulic brakes, and the bodies were generally more luxurious. Still, even the sedan was far from sluggish, being capable of 90 m.p.h. The other types were a four-passenger tourer, and the Speed Model. The latter was a 100 mp.h. car, on the short, 8 ft. 6 in. wheelbase and pulling a 4·4 : 1 axle ratio. It won its class in the 1938 Tourist Trophy Race. This type had dry-sump lubrication. So did the C-Type, developed from the Speed Model. This car, with its cowled radiator, faired-in headlamps and very long tail lacked the businesslike appearance of the Speed Model, and few were made.

82 HRG, 1936, 1938, Great Britain

E. A. Halford, G. H. Robins, and H. R. Godfrey got together in 1935 to make a new assembled sports car in the old English tradition, incorporating all that was best in it. It was a joint design. Godfrey had worked with A. Frazer-Nash on the stark and simple GN cycle-car in the days immediately before and after the First World War, but had left before Frazer-Nash went on to make a very similar sports car bearing his own name (67). The HRG, named after its promoters' initials, in fact was similar in character to the Frazer Nash, though Godfrey never had anything to do with the latter. It was an all-rounder, suitable for road trials as well as for pure speed—tough, straightforward, light and fast. The steering, brakes, and roadholding were of an extraordinarily high standard, helping to make up for the lack of outright speed in comparison with more sophisticated sports cars. At first a Meadows 4ED engine of $1\frac{1}{2}$-litres capacity was fitted; 25 of this type were built before the war. There were two carburettors. Power output rose from 50 b.h.p. in 1935 to 65 b.h.p. in 1938. The HRG differed from the chain-driven Frazer Nash mainly in its Moss-built gear-box, shaft drive and ENV live axle, and in having half-elliptic rear springs. A variety of axle ratios was to be had. The whole car, which had an aluminium body, weighed only

14½ cwt., and was capable of a rousing 92 m.p.h. in road trim on the 4 : 1 axle ratio. Stripped for racing, 100 m.p.h. could be seen. In third gear, 69 m.p.h. was available, with an acceleration time of under 11 seconds from rest to 50 m.p.h. A special version was made for the 1938 Le Mans 24-hour Race. Its engine, developing up to 75 b.h.p. was installed in a 14-cwt. body with pointed tail and cycle-type wings. An HRG was second in its class at Le Mans in 1937 and 1938, and won its class in 1939. One Triumph-engined car with a pretty coupé body was built in 1938 (lower illustration), but in the following year eight of a new type were made. It differed from the Meadows car in having the 1100 c.c. overhead-camshaft engine out of the contemporary Singer Nine, slightly modified to give up to 40 b.h.p. at 4800 r.p.m. There was a Singer synchromesh gear-box, and a 4·55 : 1 axle ratio. The 1100, and the bigger car also now with a Singer engine, were made after the Second World War, lasting until 1956, by which time the HRG's naked radiator, unadorned by any grille, and its beam front axle were real anachronisms.

83   **SINGER LE MANS
        REPLICA,** 1936,
        Great Britain

The pedigree of one of the best and most successful small, cheap sports cars characteristic of Britain in the 1930s dated back to 1927, when Singer attacked the really low-priced light-car market dominated by the Austin Seven, with their Junior. The little four-cylinder engine of 847 c.c. had a single

chain-driven overhead camshaft and developed 16½ b.h.p. at 3250 r.p.m. There were three forward speeds. The Junior proved immensely popular, and a mildly sporting version, the Porlock, joined it. In 1932 the 8-h.p. Junior was replaced by the Nine, of basically similar design but with a bigger cylinder bore. The following year saw the first sports model Nine, capable of 65 m.p.h. with the standard four-passenger body. It won a Coupe des Glaciers for a clean sheet in the 1932 International Alpine Trial. In 1933, and every year until 1939 except 1936, when the race was not held, Singers were entered in the Le Mans 24-hour Race. They never did startlingly well, but were consistent performers, coming in ninth on the Index of Performance in 1935 and seventh in 1938. The French agent for the make, Jacques Savoye, was an enthusiastic competitor. The result, for 1934, was the introduction of the famous Le Mans Special Speed Model Singer. The two-carburettor engine developed 40 b.h.p. at 4700 r.p.m. and was safe up to 6000 r.p.m., thanks to the two-bearing but short and very stiff crankshaft. This, the Lockheed hydraulic brakes, the synchromesh gear-box, and the Singer's superior roadholding gave it an edge over the contemporary P-type MG, its main competitor. Maximum speed, at 75 m.p.h., was about the same, and as in the MG, the gearing was very low— 5·57 : 1—to cope with hills in sporting trials. Two- or four-passenger bodies were offered, the former being in the classic fashionable style with cutaway doors, slab fuel tank, and cycle-type wings. The 1935 Le Mans works cars were serious road-racing cars with light, long-tailed two-passenger bodies and a maximum speed of 90 m.p.h., on the 4·77 : 1 top gear ratio. Seventy-five m.p.h. was available in third gear, and over 60 in second, thanks to a close-ratio gear-box. As the Le Mans Replica, this type was listed alongside the normal Le Mans model in 1936.

was dropped in 1950, when it ceased to be available, and the 4/4 too, disappeared for five years. It was reborn as the Series II 4/4 in 1955, with a side-valve Ford Ten unit out of the last three-wheeler, the F4 Morgan, which had been made until 1950. Later came an overhead-valve 105E Ford engine.

84 MORGAN 4/4, 1936–9, Great Britain

This excellent little sports car, introduced in 1936, was Morgan's first four-wheeler, leaving aside experimental models (30, 31). A four-cylinder engine was not so new, having been offered in the traditional three-wheeler since 1933, when a Ford unit was used, but the car's sliding-pillar independent front suspension had been seen on all Morgans since the first of 1910. As usual, too, the engine was a proprietary unit, in this case made by Coventry-Climax and developing 36 b.h.p. at 4500 r.p.m. The 4/4 weighed only 13 cwt., so this modest power output provided 75 m.p.h., which was allied to good handling, as one might expect. The separate gear-box was a conservative but classic feature of British sports cars. For 1938, a four-passenger model was introduced, and for 1939, a coupé was added. Morgans finished thirteenth and fourteenth at Le Mans in 1938 and 1939 respectively. The rather earlier Sandford from France, offered by a firm that had started by making cars to the Morgan three-wheeler formula, was on similar lines, with its 1100 c.c. four-cylinder Ruby engine. In 1939 an all-overhead-valve 1267 c.c. Standard Ten engine was substituted. This unit

85 MG TA MIDGET, 1936–9, Great Britain

After 1935, the traditional overhead-camshaft engine of the MG Midget was dropped, and a quieter, simpler and more reliable pushrod overhead-valve type substituted. The o.h.c. Midgets had cleverly used their vertical drive-shafts to the camshaft as the dynamo armature, but this did not enhance the performance of the dynamo, into which oil penetrated. The new T series were generally less spartan cars, in keeping with the company's abandonment of competitions, their bigger, long-stroke engines less fussy, their bodies roomier and more comfortable. Power output was 50 b.h.p. at 4500 r.p.m., and the axle ratio was higher, which made them faster than the P series, although heavier at 15¾ cwt., for the TA two-passenger sports model, and they stopped better, too, with their Lockheed hydraulic brakes. A coupé was also made. About 3000 of these cars were made. During 1939, the TA was superseded by the TB type, with a shorter stroke, 1250 c.c. engine and two-passenger or coupé bodies. This, with a synchromesh gear-box, became the world-famous TC sports of post-war days.

The M45 Lagonda, new in 1933, was the first replacement for the Two-Litre (53) to establish itself. It was a car of very much the same character, in that it was a large, fast touring machine on classic British lines. The 4½-litre engine, made not by Lagonda but by Meadows, suppliers of proprietary units to many manufacturers, had in fact been designed in the 1920s by B. S. Crump, but was no worse for that, as was proved by its longevity. It was a big engine, designed to give the new car a combination of power and flexibility. Two carburettors, dual ignition and two plugs per cylinder were fitted. The brakes were servo-assisted. Power output was 105 b.h.p. The weight was a thumping 35 cwt. or 35½ cwt. for the sedan. Everything about the M45 Lagonda was heavy, including the controls. Still, the sedan could reach 92 m.p.h., and the M45 was a more obvious competition car than the old, overburdened Two-Litre. The company in 1934 introduced a more sporting version of the standard M45, the M45R or Rapide, also known as the Speed Model. This 1934/5 type had a 120 b.h.p. engine pulling a 3·3 : 1 axle ratio and 32 cwt., which was not an excessive weight for so big a car. The wheelbase, at 10 ft. 3 in., was six inches shorter than that of the normal M45, and 103 m.p.h. was available in top gear, with 82 in second and an 0–60 acceleration time of 13·2 seconds. Even the sedan could reach 100 m.p.h. The concessionaires Fox & Nicholl ran modified M45Rs; shortened cars with a higher compression ratio and higher than standard axle ratio, in the 1934 Ulster Tourist Trophy Race and the 1935 Le Mans 24-hour event. The Le Mans cars, with 150 b.h.p., a 3·14 : 1 axle and well over 100 m.p.h. on tap, won the race. In 1936, Lagondas went on to win their class in the French Grand Prix (run for sports cars), and in the Spa 24-hour Race. From 1935, W. O. Bentley (24, 25, 64) set to work redesigning the basic chassis in detail, and the 1936 cars, called L645, showed his refining influence. Without loss of performance (in spite of an increase in the weight of the normal tourer to over 35 cwt.), comfort was improved, there was synchromesh between top and third gears, and flexibility was such that a speed range of 7–97 m.p.h. in top gear was possible. On the LG45R there was a close-ratio gear-box, and lighter steering than on the M45—a much-needed improvement. The body was narrower and more cramped. The spare wheel was carried in the covered-in deck in the curved tail. Cycle-type front wings were fitted. Separate outside exhaust pipes (which also gave better extraction) completed a very sporting turnout. This was an altogether fiercer machine than the L645, lacking the refinements of remote control for the shock-absorbers, one-shot lubrication and hydraulic built-in jacks. It was a good deal lighter than the normal car, and had a more highly tuned engine, giving 130 b.h.p., and a higher axle ratio. All the LG45 range were replaced at the end of 1937 by the new LG6, a pure luxury car with independent front suspension, and by the even more exotic V12. The V12, too, was designed as a luxury car, but in this case two lighter, higher-geared, tuned examples were entered by the works in the 1939 Le Mans 24-hour Race. They took second and third places, and were capable of nearly 140 m.p.h. from what was still a 4½-litre, unsupercharged engine.

87 AC 16/80, 1936, Great Britain

The six-cylinder, 2-litre AC engine has had a remarkably long life. To be seen as late as 1963 in the AC car, this John Weller-designed unit was first used in 1919, at which time it was a very advanced design, with its chain-driven overhead camshaft, alloy block with iron cylinder liners, and aluminium pistons. Thanks to the extensive use of alloys, it was light in weight. A notably efficient design in its day, it gave plenty of scope for development. It afforded great flexibility of running to the small luxury car, the AC Six, in which it was installed. This car, at first made in only small numbers, went into serious production in 1926. Complete redesign in the early 1930s followed a change in control of the company, since 1930 in the hands of the brothers W. A. E. and C. F. Hurlock. By that time, apart from the half-elliptic springs which had been substituted in 1930, only the engine was still modern. Otherwise the chassis for 1933 was completely new, with a dropped frame, and a four-speed gearbox in the normal position instead of the earlier, three-speed unit on the back axle. This basic chassis was called the Ace, of which, at this period, the engine developed 56 b.h.p. However, a 66 b.h.p. engine was available in 1933; with three carburettors. The sports sedan of 1934 was so powered. It weighed 25 cwt. and had a gear-box

with fairly close ratios, and a 4·66 : 1 axle ratio. The 0–50 acceleration time was 16 seconds, and 0–60, 20 seconds. Maximum speed was just under 80 m.p.h. For 1936 there came, alongside it, a short-chassis open car, the 16/80 h.p., with greater power and a 4·5 : 1 axle, and capable of 85 m.p.h. The sports coupé version weighed just over a ton, and pulled a 4·25 : 1 or 4·5 : 1 axle ratio, which gave it a maximum of 85 m.p.h. and an 0–50 time of 12·2 seconds. From rest to 60 m.p.h. occupied 18·1 seconds. In 1937 came the lighter, shorter 16/80 h.p. Ace Competition, with a still higher compression, 80 b.h.p., the 4·25 : 1 axle, and 88 m.p.h. The Ace Competition could be had in its fiercest form as the 16/90; this, the ultimate pre-war development of the engine, was fitted with a low-pressure supercharger. The latter, unfortunately, affected reliability. Meanwhile, the old 16/56 and 16/66 designations were dropped, for 1937 and 1938, in favour of 16/60 and 16/70. Some cars had a Wilson pre-selector gearbox, but a manual change was normal. These ACs did not feature prominently as contenders in speed competitions, but they were thoroughbreds in the classic mould.

88 JENSEN S-TYPE, 1937, Great Britain

The enterprising Jensen brothers, Alan and Richard, started in the motor industry by building distinctive coachwork to be fitted to cheap chassis that normally carried unimaginative factory bodies. This was in 1928, when many firms were taking advantage of popular demand in this way. That year, when they made a special body for an Austin Seven, they were barely out of their teens. They went on to design the famous Avon bodies for Standards (32), Wolseley, Ford, and Morris. Like William Lyons (98), the Jensen brothers progressed to building their own cars, starting for 1937 with a machine they named after themselves. In part, the Jensen used proprietary components, such as a Ford V8 engine, tuned to give 120 b.h.p. and 85 m.p.h. in the case of the sports tourer and over 80 m.p.h. in the 31-cwt. sedan and convertible, but the very stiff, boxed, braced chassis, the suspension, servo-assisted brakes, and steering were Jensen products, so as to take care of the car's handling qualities. A two-speed rear axle was fitted, effectively providing six forward speeds. The final drive ratio was 4·11 : 1, or 2·9 : 1. This S-type Jensen was current from 1937 until 1939. It was joined for 1938 by a car with the smaller Ford V8 engine of 2227 c.c. supercharged, and a shorter wheelbase. The S-type was supplemented by the Model H, which had an in-line eight-cylinder overhead-valve engine made by Nash with 4·2 litres but about the same power output, delivered in a much more refined manner. The frame was heavier than that of the S-type, but performance was about the same. The 34-cwt. sedan could accelerate from rest to 50 m.p.h. in 10·4 seconds, could attain 95 m.p.h., and cruised at 85 m.p.h. on the higher of the two top gears. There was independent front suspension, by coil springs and wishbones. This car became the Model HC of 1939. At the same time, surprisingly for so small a concern, experiments were made with commercial vehicles. After the Second World War, the Model HC, with coil spring independent suspension at the rear, was produced.

89 BROUGH SUPERIOR, 1936–40, Great Britain

George Brough was already famous for making one of the finest motor-cycles ever built, the Brough Superior, when in 1935 he diversified into cars. Initially Brough Superior Cars of Nottingham chose the eight-cylinder Hudson unit of 4 litres' capacity used in the Railton (72), a car of very similar character and intention. However, the production Broughs of 1936–40 fitted the six-cylinder Hudson engine of $3\frac{1}{2}$ litres, tuned to give 107 b.h.p., with an aluminium cylinder-head and other alterations. The handling and stability of these cars was of a high order, thanks to Lockheed hydraulic brakes, light, high-geared steering, and the location of the front axle by radius arms. The axle ratio was 4·1 : 1. Sedan and convertible bodies were fitted, the 26-cwt. convertible being capable of over 90 m.p.h. (lower illustration). In quite a different class, however, was the Alpine (upper illustration), an uncompromisingly sporting car, with a supercharged engine that developed 140 b.h.p. (This could also be had in the convertible.) The very stark two-passenger body weighed only 110 lb. Thanks to an all-up weight of only 21 cwt., and a 3·56 : 1 axle ratio, maximum speed was well in excess of 100 m.p.h., and the acceleration was fabulous. From rest to 50 m.p.h. occupied 7·2 seconds, and rest to

60 m.p.h. 9·8 seconds. The top-gear acceleration was even more startling, 20–70 occupying a mere 16 seconds. At the opposite extreme was a luxury car with which Brough toyed in 1938. This had a special chassis designed for it from scratch, owing nothing to American practice, underslung at the rear and very rigid. The power unit was the vee-twelve Lincoln Zephyr of 4·4 litres, giving 112 b.h.p. in the Brough, and a top speed of around 80 m.p.h. Girling mechanical brakes were fitted, and the body was made by Charlesworth. It seems likely that only one of these cars was built, leaving the six to carry the flag.

90 MERCEDES-BENZ 540K, 1937–9, Germany

After the demise of the S series in 1931 (17), Daimler-Benz made no more true sports cars before the Second World War. High-speed touring machines such as the Mannheim 370S Sport (43) and the 380K of 1932–3, with sporting lines and in some cases greater maximum speed, acceleration and technical sophistication than the real thing, were the order of the day from Stuttgart as from most other German manufacturers; they were designed for sustained *autobahn*-burning, not twisty competition courses, but in spite of their quite different handling characteristics, they had enough in common with sports cars to deserve inclusion here, and the manufacturers used the word 'sport' in their designations, at least when the bodies justified it. The 3·8-litre 380K, producing 90 b.h.p. unblown and 120 b.h.p. blown, was the first Mercedes-Benz to offer the combination of eight cylinders, independent suspension all round and hydraulic brakes. It was succeeded by the 500K in the same line of development. The massive frame was probably identical. The weight was $48\frac{1}{2}$ cwt. for the four-passenger cabriolet, and the steering was slow and heavy, but the 500K's 5-litre engine developed 100 b.h.p. at 3400 r.p.m. running unsupercharged and 160 b.h.p. with blower engaged, which in conjunction with a 3·03 : 1 overdrive top gear meant 85 m.p.h. and 102 m.p.h. respectively. Fuel consumption was 11 m.p.g. In 1937 this great car was superseded by the 540K, which is illustrated. A slightly bigger engine offered 180 b.h.p. at 3300 r.p.m. supercharged and 115 b.h.p. unsupercharged, but weight had risen to over 49 cwt., and the top-gear ratio had gone down to 3·9 : 1, so the maximum speed rose only to 88 and 106 m.p.h. However, 75 m.p.h. instead of only 60 was now obtainable in third gear, the steering was less heavy, and the car was quieter and more comfortable. Limousines and sedans as well as the more common cabriolets were built. The model was made until 1939, when at the Berlin Show, the car that was to have succeeded it, the 580K, was displayed. It never went into production.

91 HANSA 1700 and 1700 SPORT, 1937, Germany

Like so many other European manufacturers, Hansa during the later 1920s built cars of conventional American type, with six- or eight-cylinder

Continental-made engines and Lockheed hydraulic brakes. The first step away from purely pedestrian design was taken in 1931, with the introduction of the Matador, which had independent rear suspension by swing axles. Carl F. W. Borgward had assumed control of the Hansa Automobilwerke AG in 1929, and the first of a really modern, Borgward-inspired series of cars appeared in 1934. There was a rear-engined, two-stroke, two-cylinder utility model with backbone frame and all-independent suspension called the 500, and (less ephemeral), a front-engined 1100 c.c. machine with four cylinders, also with backbone frame and independent suspension. The engine developed 28 b.h.p., giving the car a maximum of 60 m.p.h., and the roadholding was good. It was current until 1939. A six with two more cylinders of the same dimensions, the 1700, was made alongside it. The engine produced 40 b.h.p. at 3800 r.p.m., which gave a top speed of 65 m.p.h. There was a four-speed synchromesh gear-box, and hydraulic brakes. The basic design lent itself to sporting work, particularly in respect of the roadholding, and the little-known 1700 Sport of 1935–7 followed. It had a 50 b.h.p. engine with twin carburettors. Maximum speed was around 75 m.p.h. Very few were made, and the handful of sports cars made in Germany at this time were quite overshadowed by the remarkable Type 328 BMW (75). The 2000 model Hansa of 1937–8 used a 2-litre engine in the same chassis. Experiments were carried out with a twin overhead-camshaft engine turning at 7000 r.p.m. in an aerodynamic body, for which car 125 m.p.h. was claimed.

92 BMW TYPE 319/1, 1937, Germany

The first cars of the Bayerische Motorenwerke AG were derived from the British Austin Seven via the French Rosengart, and were not technically remarkable in any way. Indeed they were too heavy for their chassis. In 1932 there arrived a technical revolution in the shape of the first home-grown BMW design, by Fritz Fiedler, and this, as far as the chassis was concerned, was anything but conventional. The power unit was a small overhead-valve four, installed in a tubular frame with all-independent suspension by swing axles. The bodies were built by Mercedes-Benz. This 3/20 h.p. was an interim design. At the 1933 Berlin Show, there appeared the first of a long and illustrious line of Fiedler-designed six-cylinder cars, equipped with a completely new engine as well as an advanced chassis. This Type 303 had a 1200 c.c. engine and tubular frame, retaining independent front suspension though dropping independent rear suspension, a very modern layout contrasting with the traditional combination of whippy chassis and stiff leaf-spring suspension. The 303 was enlarged into the 1490 c.c. Type 315 of 1934–6. Its engine developed 34 b.h.p. at 4000 r.p.m. It was clear by now that the Fiedler design, with its practical combination of fine acceleration, high top speed, excellent steering and roadholding, light weight, smoothness and flexibility of running, economy, low price and roominess, provided the ideal basis for a new breed of civilized sports car that could combine the virtues of the fiercer class of vehicle with those of the family sedan. (In fact the later BMW sedans used a more normal steel-box type of frame, not the tubular affair, but it, too, was very stiff). The 315/1 sports model gave 40 b.h.p. and 78 m.p.h. The performance of BMWs in the 1934 and 1935 International Alpine Trials, where they won their class, helped induce the Aldington brothers, whose company A.F.N. Ltd made the Frazer Nash (51), to import and assemble the German car as the Frazer Nash-BMW. The 315/1 sports was known in England as the Type 40, from its power output. A further development was the Type 319 of 1936-8, which had 65 × 96 mm. cylinder dimensions giving 1911 c.c., and in normal form produced 45 b.h.p. at 3750 r.p.m. The sports version, that illustrated, weighed only $14\frac{3}{4}$ cwt., and with three carburettors and 55 b.h.p. at 4000 r.p.m. offered an 83-m.p.h. maximum on the 3·9 : 1 axle ratio. It took a mere 15·2 seconds to accelerate from rest to 60 m.p.h., yet returned 26 m.p.g. This car was sold as the Type 55 in England. The ultimate refinement of the BMW sports series, the Type 328, is discussed under (75).

93 CORD 812, 1937, U.S.A.

Gordon Buehrig, chief body designer of Duesenberg Inc. (62) in late 1933 began work on a lower-priced Duesenberg for a less-prosperous market than that which was buying the great Model J and SJ, to suit the depressed times. In fact Buehrig moved to Auburn (66) before his new design could appear, and when it did so, late in 1935, it was as a new Cord, with front-wheel drive. This Cord 810 was a remarkable vehicle by any standards of the time, and particularly so in America, where rationalization in the motor industry had progressed further than anywhere else. The car's smooth lines were accentuated by its disappearing headlamps and its lack of a conventional radiator grille. The prototype had two radiators, one on either side between wing and hood. Instead of a grille, there were long horizontal louvres which wrapped around the hood. Unitary construction of body and chassis was employed, and there was independent front suspension. The all-indirect gears were pre-selected by a vacuum servo-operated electric shift. There were four forward speeds, but normal motoring was done in third, for top was a specially geared-up cruising ratio. The Lycoming engine had eight cylinders, in 90 degree vee formation, with a counterbalanced crankshaft. It developed 125 b.h.p. at 3500 r.p.m. Naturally, this very advanced machine carried a price to match—double that of the contemporary Cadillac, in fact. In 1937 the 810 was developed into the 812, in which the main differences were an optional supercharger and long chassis for more formal bodies. In unblown form, the 812 sedan weighing 35 cwt. was capable of 90 m.p.h., with 86 in third, and an acceleration figure of 0-60 m.p.h. in 20 seconds. The cruising speed was 80-85, on the 2·75 : 1 high ratio. The 812 speedster, with supercharger, could reach 110 m.p.h. with its 170 b.h.p. engine. On later cars, this output was increased to 195 b.h.p. at 4200 r.p.m. The surprisingly high number of 2320 810 and 812 Cords were built before the end of the Cord Corporation in 1937 brought about their demise.

94 BUGATTI TYPE 57SC,
1937–8, France

The Type 57 Bugatti of 1934 was a touring design intended to replace the Type 49 introduced in 1930. This, in turn, had been a development of the straight-eight, single-camshaft, twenty-four valve Type 44, which had been Bugatti's first successful attempt to make a truly refined, but still fast, touring car. The Type 57 was in natural succession to these fine cars, with its combination of quiet, smooth tractability with high power, but technically it belonged to the line of new twin overhead-camshaft, sixteen-valve, straight-eights launched with the Type 51 Grand Prix car of 1931 and the Type 55 sports version of 1932 (52)—though with plain instead of roller bearings. It was, however, a more docile, civilized machine than the latter—better though the Type 55 had been in these respects than its own predecessors. Initially, it was not a sports car at all, though its performance outshone that of most contemporary sporting vehicles. Chassis weight was only 19 cwt., and with the standard engine developing 125 b.h.p. at 4500 r.p.m., even the $27\frac{1}{2}$-cwt. sedan was capable of up to 95 m.p.h., with 75 m.p.h. in third gear. Handling was superb, as might be expected from a Bugatti. The Type 57 and its variants were so successful that they were the sole Bugatti production cars until war

came in 1939. Refinements were added over the years—rubber engine mountings and De Ram shock-absorbers in 1936 (though the latter were replaced by simpler, cheaper hydraulic dampers in 1938), Lockheed hydraulic brakes, a quieter engine and a stiffer frame in 1938. The Type 57 might be a touring car, but it had great sporting potential which was quickly exploited. One was the fastest car in the 1935 Ulster Tourist Trophy Race, and from 1936 until 1938 the so-called Competition Model or 57S (Sport) was listed. The frame of this car was shortened, stiffened and lowered, there was divided-axle front suspension, and dry-sump lubrication and a stronger clutch helped cope with an increase of power to 175 b.h.p. at 5500 r.p.m. With streamlined bodies, cars of this type won the 1936 French Grand Prix (a sports-car race that year), and also the 1937 Le Mans 24-hour Race. In 1937–8 there was listed the still fiercer Type 57SC, this being a supercharged 57S, the C standing for *compresseur*. The Roots-type supercharger provided 200 b.h.p. and 130 m.p.h. More 'touring' was the Type 57C made in 1938, which was the normal Type 57 with supercharger. It combined violent but silent acceleration with great flexibility. Its engine produced 160 b.h.p., which propelled the sedan at 105 m.p.h. The special 57C that won the 1939 Le Mans Race was capable of 150 m.p.h. or more. About 725 of all variations on the Type 57 theme were made. Its would-be successors, the pre-war Type 64 and the post-war Type 101 (fundamentally a Type 57 with a Cotal electric gear-box) never went into production.

95 TALBOT-LAGO, 1937, France

Until 1935, the English Clement-Talbot and Sunbeam companies, together with Automobiles Talbot in France, had formed the Sunbeam-Talbot-Darracq combine. In England, to avoid confusion with the English Talbot (49), the French Talbot was called a Darracq. In the year mentioned, the English companies were taken over by the Rootes brothers, who already controlled Hillman and Humber. Major Antoine F. Lago, owner of Automobiles Talbot, launched an independent policy akin to that of Delahaye (79), concentrating on luxurious prestige cars of high performance and modern design that could be, and were to be, adapted for serious competition work. The new machine, starting life in 1936, was called a Talbot-Lago in France, and (as before) a Darracq in England, where Rootes were still making Talbot cars. The 4-litre 23CV engine had hemispherical combustion chambers, thanks to inclined overhead valves operated from a single low camshaft by unequal-length cross-pushrods. Power output was 105 b.h.p., or 165 b.h.p. at 4200 r.p.m., in the case of the Lago Special engine, the most powerful. Independent front suspension was used. Talbot-Lagos won the 1937 French Grand Prix, the 1937 Tourist Trophy Race at Donington Park, and the 1938 Monte Carlo Rally. Post-war engines had two high (not overhead) camshafts, with inclined valves operated through rockers and short pushrods, and a cubic capacity of 4485 c.c. (93 × 110 mm.). This engine developed 170 b.h.p. A Talbot-Lago won the Le Mans 24-hour Race in 1950, and there was also a single-seater Grand Prix car using the same basic layout.

96 RILEY SPRITE, 1937, Great Britain

In 1934 and 1935, Riley Ltd offered a six-cylinder sports car, the MPH, alongside the four-cylinder Imp (68). This machine had a developed form of the 14/6 engine introduced in 1928, and was based on the six-cylinder "Grebes" Riley ran in the 1933 Ulster Tourist Trophy Race. It was elegant as well as a purposeful car, strongly reminiscent of the almost contemporary 8C 2300 Alfa-Romeos (51), and was altogether more formidable than the Imp, with an 85 m.p.h. maximum in standard trim. With the normal Riley stroke of 95·2 mm., it could be had with varying bores giving cubic capacities of between 1458 c.c. and 1726 c.c. at different times. An MPH won its class at Le Mans in 1934, while the company offered special components to make racing engines out of the normal six-cylinder units. The racing six of Raymond Mays, the 'White Riley', was the basis for the ERA racing car. However, the MPH was dropped in 1935, and a new four-cylinder car, the Sprite, introduced in its place in 1936. This was a spendid machine, better than either the Imp or the MPH. The 1½-litre engine, adapted from the 12/4 unit in use in a touring Riley, would turn at 5000 r.p.m. In its basic form, the engine had been introduced for 1935. It was an improvement on the trusty Nine unit (27), which had been redesigned by Hugh Rose and given three main bearings.

Weight was not excessive—an unusual virtue in the middle 1930s—and 90 m.p.h. was to be had, in spite of a wide-ratio Wilson pre-selector gear-box: although the final drive ratio was a somewhat depressing 5·22 : 1. Wheelbase was the same as the MPH: 8 ft. $1\frac{1}{2}$ in., for the chassis was that of the MPH, with modifications. The Sprite was available in more exciting Ulster Sprite form. Freddie Dixon's $1\frac{1}{2}$-litre 4-cylinder Rileys won the 1935 and 1936 Tourist Trophy races. The 12/4 engine, ancestor of all these exciting power units, was the most successful ever installed in a Riley.

97 ALTA TWO LITRE, 1938–9, Great Britain

Geoffrey Taylor's Altas, like the contemporary Maseratis, were available as both pure racing cars and as sports-racing cars (50), being basically the same cars in different stages of tune and with or without road equipment. After making tuning modifications for the Austin Seven, including aluminium high-compression cylinder heads, from about 1927, Taylor started to build cars of his own design in about 1930. All were of the same design. The engines had four cylinders in an alloy block with iron liners and an alloy cylinder-head, two overhead camshafts, gear-driven, hemispherical combustion chambers and efficient breathing, running with a Roots-type supercharger or unsupercharged. Altas were very low-built, with underslung front half-elliptic springs and quarter-elliptics at the rear. At first a normal manual gear-box was supplied but later cars usually

had the Wilson pre-selector mechanism. The first Altas were of 1100 c.c., developing 68 b.h.p. at 6000 r.p.m. unblown. They were good for 100 m.p.h. supercharged. The 1500 c.c. cars, supercharged, produced 120 b.h.p. at 5700 r.p.m., and were capable of upwards of 115 m.p.h. They arrived in 1935, together with the biggest, two-litre model, which is illustrated. It was invariably supercharged, and offered 180 b.h.p. The car shown illustrates the dual rôle of all Altas. It is a road-equipped two-seater, but has the independent front suspension of the post-1937 pure racing types.

98 SS100, 1938, 1939, Great Britain

Having made a success of his Swallow sidecars for motor-cycles, William Lyons turned to building specially distinctive bodies for pedestrian family cars that in production form wore heavy, ugly coachwork. In this he catered for a growing demand of the late 1920s, when the mass production of cheap cars meant that a new uniformity was the rule. Like the Jensen brothers and others (88), but earlier, Lyons next went on to making his own cars, or rather, having the parts built for him and then putting them together himself. His first SS, as he called it, appeared in 1932 and was based on the side-valve 1100 c.c. 9 h.p., 2-litre 16 h.p. and $2\frac{1}{2}$-litre 20 h.p. Standards. The components were supplied by the big Coventry firm to Lyons' special specifications. Lyons and the SS had many affinities with Errett Lobban Cord and the Auburn (66). Lyons' recipe was a shrewd combination of exceptionally rakish elegance (achieved mainly by means of an underslung frame and the very low line this permitted), with robust simplicity, ready availability of spare parts and service, a very high standard of finish and a low price. These were good cars, with a better performance than the Standard products thanks to mildly-tuned engines and higher axle ratios, but they strove for sporting effect, not for true sporting character. More serious things were to come. The 20 h.p. four-passenger sports tourer of 1933 disposed of 62 b.h.p. Its successor the SS90 two-passenger sports car of 1935 had a higher state of tune and a higher final drive ratio. In that year came the first of the new SS Jaguars, with an overhead-valve cylinder-head designed by Harry Weslake. The $2\frac{1}{2}$-litre engine gave 104 b.h.p., which sufficed to propel the sedan at 90 m.p.h. This car, unlike its predecessor, provided a first-class basis for a true sports model, which duly accompanied it. This SS100 was a light machine, firmly sprung, with high-geared steering and well-chosen gear ratios, on a shorter chassis than the sedan. Power output was 115 b.h.p. at 4500 r.p.m. Maximum speed was over 90 m.p.h., with an acceleration time from rest to 60 m.p.h. of $13\frac{1}{2}$ seconds. The weight distribution was not very good, so the tail ran 'light' and handling at speed was tricky, but the SS100, with its speed, stunning good looks and low price was an exceedingly popular car. In 1938 it was joined by a larger-engined model, the $3\frac{1}{2}$-litre SS100 (upper illustration), which arrived once a touring car of similar engine size became available. Power output was

boosted to 125 b.h.p. at 4250 r.p.m., which provided 106 m.p.h. with refinement, and 86 m.p.h. in third gear. The time from rest to 60 m.p.h. was down to 10·4 seconds. A fixed-head coupé (lower illustration) and a convertible were listed in 1939 and 1940 respectively, but none was sold. Before the Second World War the company did not seriously go in for speed competitions, but an SS100 $2\frac{1}{2}$-litre won its class in the International Alpine Trial of 1936.

99 BRITISH SALMSON
20/90, 1938, Great Britain

British Salmson Aero Engines Ltd were the British associates of the Société des Moteurs Salmson of Billancourt, who had been famous in the 1920s for their small sports cars and were now making more pedestrian, if more civilized, fast touring machinery. The British company turned to cars in 1934, with a four-cylinder, twin overhead-camshaft, $1\frac{1}{2}$-litre vehicle that was virtually the S4C Salmson with an English body. In touring form it was called the 12/55, the second figure being the claimed brake horsepower. The 12/70 was the sports version, with a maximum of over 85 m.p.h. pulling the 4·75 : 1 axle ratio. This was creditable, for all British Salmsons were heavy cars, though beautifully made. The very rigid chassis was sprung by half-elliptics at the front and quarter-elliptic springs at the rear. A new, six-cylinder model of 1936 was entirely British in origin as far as the engine went, though retaining the same stroke (with a larger bore), the twin o.h.c. layout, and the French car's Saint

Andrew's Cross on the radiator. The twin-carburettor 20/90 sports engine developed 90 b.h.p. at 4500 r.p.m. The chassis was the same as that of the four-cylinder car, except that there was independent front suspension. Maximum speed was over 90 m.p.h. Production of British Salmsons ceased in 1939, by which time its manufacturers were only importing French Salmsons.

100 ATALANTA 1½ LITRE, 1938, Great Britain

The Atalanta was a distinctive specialist machine made by Atalanta Motors Ltd of Staines, Middlesex, in small numbers between 1937 and 1939. The exceptionally interesting specification embraced four-wheel independent suspension, exceedingly rare in a land of conventional sports cars, a very rigid frame, electron brake drums and crankcase, and the option of an American Warner four-speed gear-box with freewheel, or a Cotal electric gear-box. Outwardly the Atalanta was distinguished by its outside exhaust pipes. The engines installed in these beautifully made machines were equally unusual except in one case. Designed by Albert Gough, formerly of Frazer-Nash (67), the smallest, 1½-litre unit had an overhead camshaft and three valves per cylinder. It developed no less than 78 b.h.p. and was understandably somewhat rough. One of these cars ran in the Le Mans 24-hour Race in 1938, without success. There was also a 2-litre with 98 b.h.p. engine, and a very low, handsome, compact vee-twelve powered by the American side-valve

Lincoln Zephyr engine. In its original form this unit developed 110 b.h.p., but mildly tuned in the Atalanta, gave 112 b.h.p. at 3900 r.p.m. from 4·4 litres. A supercharger was optional. The vee-twelve on the short, 9 ft. chassis was a 100 m.p.h. machine, pulling an axle ratio of 3·6 : 1. There were three forward speeds.

101 ALFA-ROMEO 8C 2900B, 1938, Italy

The Alfa-Romeo company failed in 1933, through trying to make cars of too limited appeal at too high prices. After reorganization, 1934 saw the introduction of a six-cylinder, twin-camshaft series that reflected a radical change of policy, away from the wealthy sportsman towards a wider market, with cars that were cheaper to build. To encourage the former, they had freewheel and synchromesh, softer suspension and a less tricky gear-change, were easier to maintain, and wore a radiator grille as a concession to modern styling. They were sound, reliable cars that would have stood up to most comparisons, except with their own predecessors. The 6C 2300A of 1934—except in lightened, shortened Pescara form—was a pedestrian motor-car, and it was replaced by the 6C 2300B, which had independent suspension all round, a rigid frame, and hydraulic brakes. The 6C 2300A won the Targa Abruzzo Race in 1934, 1935, and 1937, and the 6C 2300B won in 1938. The latter model was developed into the 6C 2500 of 1939, which in its hottest, 150 b.h.p. form won the 1939 Mille

Miglia. Still, these 6C cars never achieved the réclame of their fore-runners. This was left to a very different, if tiny and commercially insignificant series of machines to do. The company found themselves in 1935 with 32 spare 2·9-litre engines left over from the obsolete *monoposto* Type B (P3) Grand Prix car. These were detuned, and installed into the 6C 2300B chassis, modified in respect of added stiffening, and swing-axle and transverse-leaf rear independent suspension instead of swing axles and torsion bars. The gear-box was in unit with the rear axle. The 1935 Mille Miglia was won by what was virtually a Type B Grand Prix car with road equipment; the prototype of the new series. The first catalogued version was the 8C 2900A of 1936, with 220 b.h.p. engine, of which six were made. This type won the 1936 Mille Miglia and Spa 24-hour Race. The 8C 2900B of 1937 had an 180 b.h.p. engine. It came in two chassis lengths, both carrying two-passenger bodies only. The 8C 2900B won the 1937 and 1947 Mille Miglia races. In Mille Miglia form, with 4·16 : 1 axle ratio and weighing only 25 cwt., this Alfa-Romeo was one of the world's fastest catalogued cars, with a maximum speed of nearly 140 m.p.h. The manu-facturer's claim of up to 118 m.p.h. for a car with the 4·54 : 1 axle was distinctly modest, since they were known to attain 130 mp.h. The cars illustrated are (above), a 1938 Mille Miglia machine and (below) a Le Mans car of the same

year. The latter would not look out of place in the 1960s.

102 RAYMOND MAYS,
1939, Great Britain

Raymond Mays, the eminent racing driver who had turned constructor with his ERA racing cars, and who was to be responsible for the BRM in post-war days, decided to attack the sports-car market in 1939. The machine that was named after him was handsome and comfortable, but lacked the per-formance of otherwise similar vehicles (72, 88, 89), because it was not based on American engines, which were more powerful, yet leisurely and reliable. Mays' starting-point was the current vee-eight Standard, which had an excellent engine developing 75 b.h.p. at 4000 r.p.m. This gave the Standard an acceleration time of rather over 18 seconds to 60 m.p.h. from rest, which was most creditable for a sizeable family sedan. In the Raymond Mays, the power unit gave another 10 b.h.p. at 5000 r.p.m. With a 4·75 : 1 axle ratio, it provided a maximum speed of over 90 m.p.h. The Standard gear-box was also retained. Handling was first-rate. The frame was underslung at the rear, and the independent front suspension was designed by Peter Berthon, who also had a hand in the ERA. Sedan and sports versions of the Raymond Mays were made, but only five altogether emerged from the workshops at Bourne, Lincolnshire where ERAs and BRMs were built.

INDEX

Make	*Model*	*Ref. No.* (colour)	*Page No.* (description)
A.C.	16/80	87	169
Adler	Trumpf Sport	76	160
Adler	Trumpf Junior Sport	77	160
Alfa-Romeo	6C1750GS	42	136
Alfa-Romeo	8C2300 Monza	51	143
Alfa-Romeo	8C2900B	101	178
Alta	Two Litre	97	176
Alvis	FWD	29	127
Alvis	12/60	48	140
Alvis	SA Speed 20	54	145
Amilcar	CGSs	4	111
Aries	3 Litre Sport	23	123
Aston Martin	Le Mans	56	146
Aston Martin	Speed Model	81	165
Atalanta	$1\frac{1}{2}$ Litre	100	178
Auburn	Model 851 Speedster	66	153
Austin	Seven Super Sports	13	116
Austin	Ulster	13	116
Austin	Seven Nippy	71	157
Austin	Seven Speedy	71	157
Austro-Daimler	ADM 111	2	109
Austro-Daimler	ADR Sport	18	120
Austro-Daimler	ADR 6 Bergmeister	19	120
Bentley	$4\frac{1}{2}$ Litre	24	123
Bentley	Speed Six	25	124
Bentley	$3\frac{1}{2}$ Litre	64	152
B.M.W.	Type 319/1	92	172
B.M.W.	Type 328	75	159
British Salmson	20/90	99	177
Brough Superior	1936–40	89	170
B.S.A.	3–wlr	73	159
B.S.A.	Scout	74	159
Bugatti	Type 43	10	114
Bugatti	Type 55	52	144
Bugatti	Type 57SC	94	174
Cord	L29	21	122
Cord	812	93	173

Make	Model	Ref. No. (colour)	Page No. (description)
Delage	D1S	9	114
Delage	D8SS	45	138
Delahaye	Type 135 Competition	79	162
Derby	L2 6CV	46	140
Derby	1500	47	140
Duesenberg	SJ Speedster	78	161
DuPont	Model G Le Mans	20	121
D'Yrsan	1928	8	114
Fiat	Tipo 509S	16	119
Fiat	Tipo 525S	35	130
Fiat	Tipo 525SS	35	130
Fiat	Tipo 508S	65	153
Frazer Nash	T.T. Replica	67	155
Hansa	1700	91	171
Hansa	1700 Sport	91	171
H.E.	Six	26	125
Hotchkiss	Grand Sport	80	164
H.R.G.	1936, 1938	82	165
Invicta	$4\frac{1}{2}$ Litre Type S	40	135
Itala	Tipo 65S	15	118
Jensen	S–Type	88	169
Jordan	Speedway 8	37	132
Lagonda	Two Litre	53	144
Lagonda	Rapier	57	148
Lagonda	Rapide	86	168
Lea–Francis	Hyper Sports	28	126
Lombard	AL3	7	113
Marendaz Special	15/98	70	157
Maserati	8C–1100	50	142
Mercedes–Benz	SSK	17	119
Mercedes–Benz	370S Mannheim Sports	43	137
Mercedes–Benz	540K	90	171
M.G.	14/40	12	115
M.G.	18/100 Tigress	38	133
M.G.	M Midget	39	133
M.G.	Double Twelve Midget	39	133

Make	Model	Ref. No. (colour)	Page No. (description)
M.G.	J2 Midget	58	148
M.G.	L Magna	59	149
M.G.	K3 Magnette	60	149
M.G.	TA Midget	85	167
Minerva	AKS	36	131
Morgan	Aero	30	128
Morgan	Super Sports	31	128
Morgan	4/4	84	167
O.M.	Type 665 Superba	14	117
O.M.	2.2 Litre	41	136
Railton	Light Sports Tourer	72	158
Rally	Type ABC	11	115
Raymond Mays	1939	102	179
Riley	Brooklands	27	125
Riley	Imp	68	155
Riley	Sprite	96	175
Rolls-Royce	P I Continental	33	130
Rolls-Royce	P II Continental	34	130
S.A.R.A.	6 cyls	6	113
Simson	Supra	1	109
Singer	Le Mans Replica	83	166
Squire	1934–36	63	151
S.S.	100	98	176
Standard	Avon Special	32	129
Stutz	Black Hawk	3	110
Stutz	DV32 Bearcat	44	138
Talbot	105	49	141
Talbot-Lago	1937	95	175
Th. Schneider	10/12 CV Sport	5	112
Tracta	1929–30	22	122
Triumph Gloria	Southern Cross	69	156
Vale Special	1933–36	61	150
Wikov	Sport	62	151
Wolseley	Hornet Special	55	145